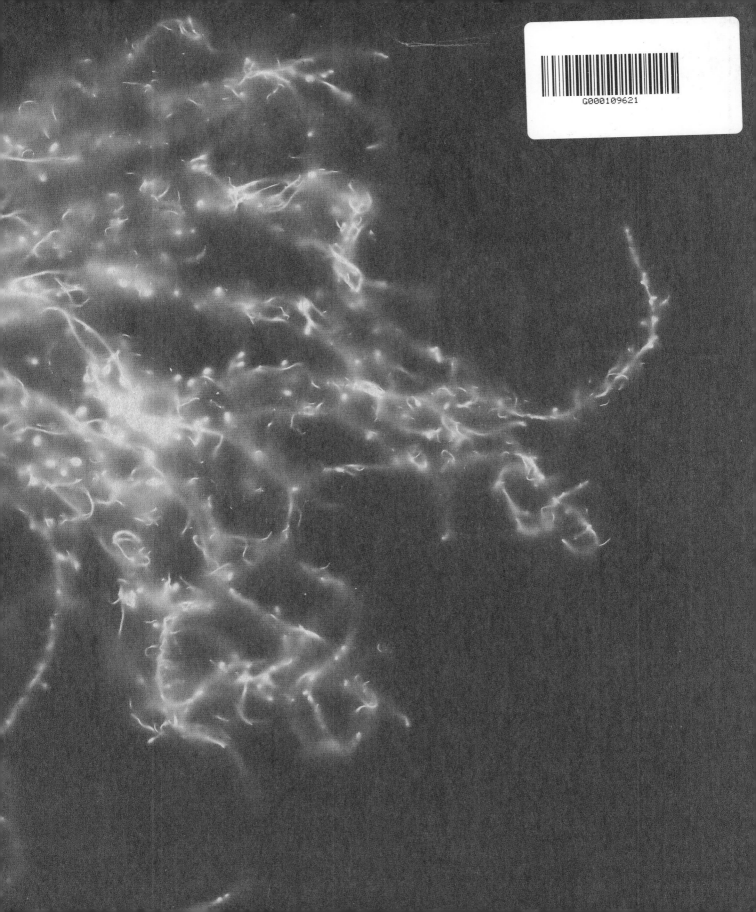

SEAWEED

A COLLECTION OF SIMPLE AND DELICIOUS RECIPES
FROM AN OCEAN OF FOOD

Claudia Seifert, Zoe Christiansen, Lisa Westgaard
& Hanne Martinsen

GRUB STREET • LONDON

CLAUDIA SEIFERT

Claudia Seifert lives in Hamburg and is a well known food stylist and cookbook writer. She is inspired by the many flavour variations found in seaweed and kelp, and she is also interested in the health benefits and the cleansing effect which the ocean's vegetables afford. You can read more about Claudia on *claudiaseifert.de.*

ZOE CHRISTIANSEN

Zoe Christiansen has a background in the arts. For the past five years she has worked with sustainability and innovation through projects such as The Future of Food and The Northern Company, which produces innovative and sustainable products using Nordic seaweed. In 2014 she received the Local EAT Award for her work with food and sustainability.

LISA WESTGAARD

Lisa Westgaard has a Bachelor of Fine Arts from the Pratt Institute, New York. After some time in New York and San Francisco, she established herself as a food and still life photographer in Oslo. Lisa works from her attic studio in Bislett. She has won several prizes for her work and is considered one of Norway's leading food photographers. See Lisa's portfolio on *tinagent.no.*

HANNE MARTINSEN

Hanne Martinsen has worked for ten years as Art Director in the advertising industry, and for the past seven years with the communication agency Dinamo. Hanne has received several honours for creativity and design, both nationally and internationally. She has been an important contributor to this publication. Hanne has conceptualised, illustrated and designed the book.

Published in 2017 by
Grub Street
4 Rainham Close
London SW11 6SS

Email: food@grubstreet.co.uk
Web: www.grubstreet.co.uk
Twitter: @grub_street
Facebook: Grub Street Publishing

Originally published in Norwegian as *Tang & Tare Et Hav Av Mat*
© CAPPELEN DAMM AS 2016
This edition is published under license of CAPPELEN DAMM AS. All rights reserved.
English translation: Anne Marie Tremlett
Cover design: Daniele Roa
Formatting English edition: Roy Platten
Landscape photography: Knut Bry / Tinagent.no
Photography: Lisa Westgaard / Tinagent.no
Author's photos: Lars Petter Pettersen / Tinagent.no
Design: Hanne Martinsen
Illustrations: Hanne Martinsen
Text: Zoe Christiansen / Henrik Berg Slang
Photo p.9: Alex Asensi and Tone Myskja
Set in 10.5 pt. Karben 105 and Minion pro

A CIP catalogue record for this book is available from the British Library.

ISBN 978-1-910690-51-2

Printed and bound by Finidr, Czech Republic

CONTENTS

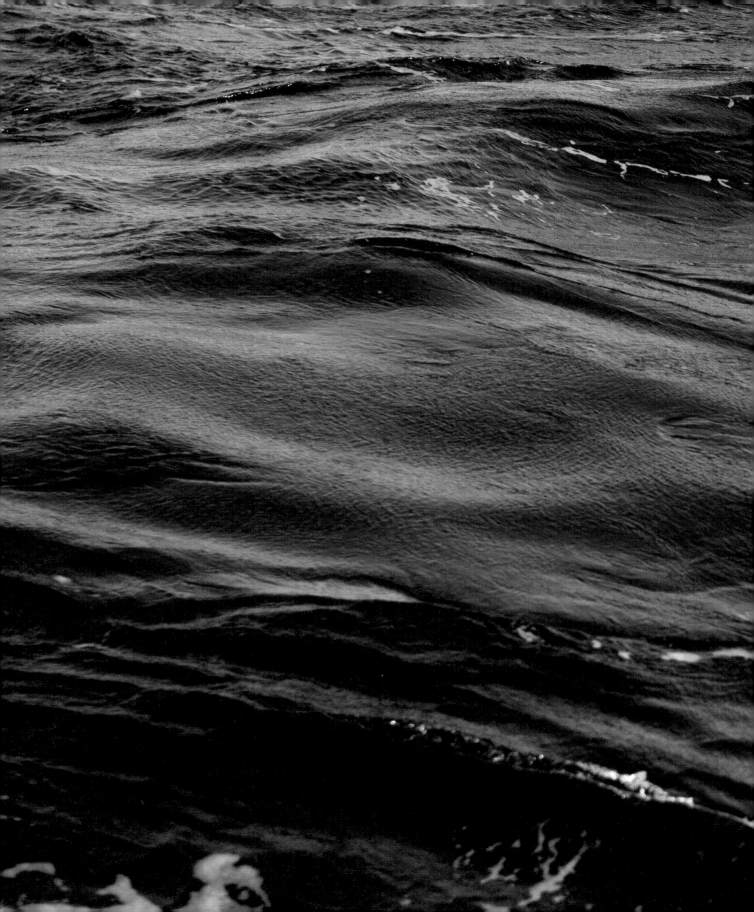

SEAWEED ON THE MENU

There are many good reasons for cooking with seaweed. Sea vegetables are not only rich in nutrients, but used correctly seaweed can lift the taste experience to another level in quite ordinary daily dishes. Seaweed is also both a sustainable and an environmentally friendly resource. On the next pages you will learn why you should cook with sea vegetables and how to go about it. We have collected 68 delicious and simple recipes using seaweed and kelp, where the ingredients have been combined with knowledge, joy and imagination.

The recipes are all different but what they have in common is that they are all simple to prepare and adapt. Thus you can quickly create a tasty meal, whether you have lunch by yourself or invite friends and family for dinner. Among the recipes you will find both main courses and snacks, soups, salads and desserts, vegetarian dishes and dishes with fish and other seafood, as well as the more experimental dishes, such as exciting tapas, quinoa risotto and gin seaweed tonic.

Enjoy!

Zoe Christiansen, Claudia Seifert, Lisa Westgaard
and Hanne Martinsen

AN OPENING TO AN OCEAN OF VEGETABLES!

All the recipes in this book are based on the most commonly available seaweed and kelp. Most of the recipes are made with dried seaweed which is available from specialist shops or the internet. But we hope that the book will inspire you also to collect the sea vegetables you want to try out. We have illustrated the different types of seaweed to make it easier for you to find the right sort of seaweed. You might also like to know, as a safety measure, that none of the sorts of seaweed that grow in Britain and Ireland are poisonous, apart from the *Desmarestia* species (there are four of them and they mostly grow in deep water) which produce sulphuric acid. Otherwise the same rules apply for harvesting seaweed and kelp as for harvesting mussels. Ideally you should pick the seaweed where the sea is in constant movement and preferably as far away as possible from housing, harbours and bathing places. The season lasts from the late winter until the early summer. Seaweed and kelp can be eaten fresh or cooked, or after having been preserved by drying, salting or maturing. If you are unable to harvest sea vegetables you can buy them quite easily.

THE FUTURE IS SEA GREEN

Transport of vegetables and protein across borders has a significant impact on the environment. In the future we will undoubtedly have to procure food using more sustainable methods. Luckily as consumers we are becoming more conscious of the environment. And this is where sea vegetables fit in perfectly: They grow locally and demand neither water, fertilisers nor additives. Seaweed and kelp are also enormously rich in nutrients. They contain a number of minerals, vitamins, trace elements and amino acids. Another point is that sea vegetables can be harvested when land vegetables have poor conditions for growth. Vegetables from the sea are a clever and sustainable supplement to ordinary vegetables grown on land.

VERSATILE USE

Sea vegetables can be used in most dishes, both as a vegetable or as a flavour enhancer. But although there are plenty of seaweed resources along coastlines, there is no tradition for using seaweed and kelp in many cuisines. We hope that this is about to change. In our work with this book we have experimented with classic recipes to give them a new twist. Most people can do this; the trick is quite simply to try different sorts of sea vegetables and learn how the various flavours and textures behave. This way you will soon find new favourites and usages. The recipes in this book are vegetarian or based on fish and shell fish, but sea vegetables also go well with meat.

ABOUT SEA VEGETABLES

Sea vegetables are used for food along the coast in many parts of the world. Seaweed and kelp are found in all the oceans of the world, almost everywhere where the sea meets land, both in deep waters and along the shore line. Underwater growths have survived for all of 500 million years without significantly changing. In the sea algae have the same function as wood, shrubs and plants have on land. All these plants ensure the production of oxygen, and have a structure which gives the basis for growth for other organisms. Seaweed and kelp are right at the bottom of the food chain and contain all the minerals the body needs – in its purest form.

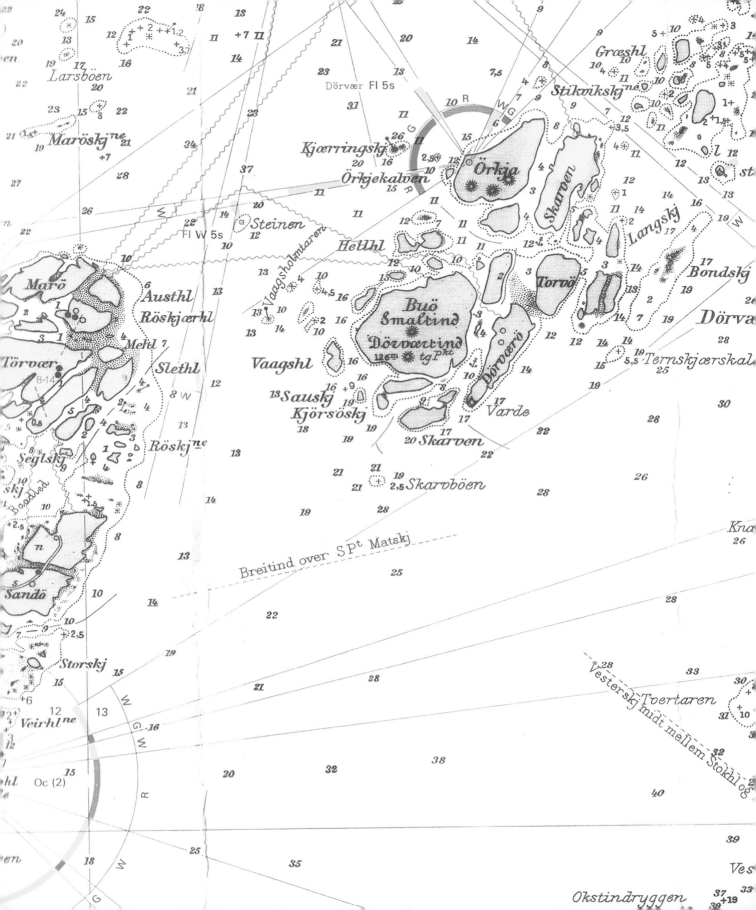

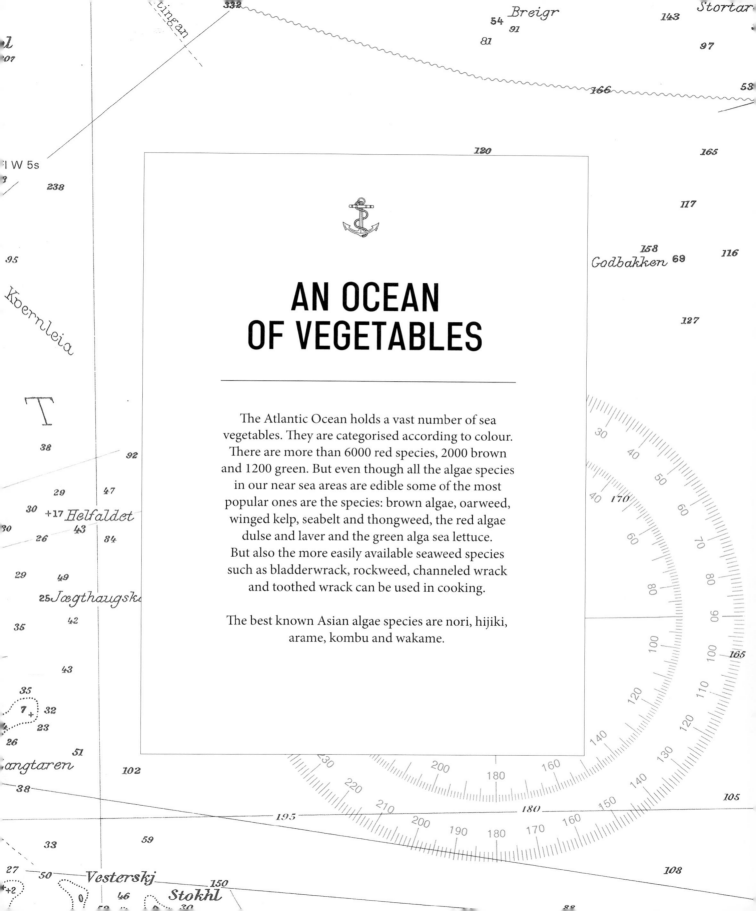

AN OCEAN OF VEGETABLES

The Atlantic Ocean holds a vast number of sea vegetables. They are categorised according to colour. There are more than 6000 red species, 2000 brown and 1200 green. But even though all the algae species in our near sea areas are edible some of the most popular ones are the species: brown algae, oarweed, winged kelp, seabelt and thongweed, the red algae dulse and laver and the green alga sea lettuce. But also the more easily available seaweed species such as bladderwrack, rockweed, channeled wrack and toothed wrack can be used in cooking.

The best known Asian algae species are nori, hijiki, arame, kombu and wakame.

HARVESTING THE SEA

Sea vegetables can only be harvested during the winter, spring and early summer before the sea becomes too warm. In areas with significant difference between ebb and flow, seaweed and kelp can be harvested at the shore line at low tide. In other areas you will need a boat or diving equipment to be able to pick the most suitable varieties.

Our tidal changes are insignificant, and we have clean water and a long coast line so these are ideal conditions for both cultivation and harvesting of sea vegetables. Sustainable cultivation of sea vegetables is now a growing source of income in several locations along our coast.

If you are harvesting seaweed you must take the same precautions as for picking mussels. Make sure that the location in the sea is in movement and that there is no habitation, industrial activity or boat traffic nearby. For the harvesting itself you will need a large basket and a pair of scissors to cut the stems. It is important that you are harvesting sustainably when you are taking wild plants.

If you are careful with cutting the seaweed a little above the stem, it will have grown out again to full size in six months time. Also make sure that you do not harvest seaweed and kelp in the same place all the time and only harvest as much as you need. They break down quickly when they have been taken out of the sea and they should be used or treated immediately after they have been taken out of their wet element.

SALT FROM THE SEA

Anyone who has a little experience with the use of seaweed in cooking can easily start with something as simple as seaweed salt. This can be purchased in specialist shops and on the internet.
But you can also make your own by drying seaweed and kelp and mixing it with sea salt flakes. This way you will also limit the salt intake and at the same time add a delicious flavour to the food and valuable nutrition. Dried seaweed can also be used as a pure substitute for salt, since it intensifies the natural salt flavour in the food. Experiment and make new versions of traditional dishes lower in salt.

STOCK

If you want to use seaweed and kelp in everyday cooking you can make a seaweed stock. The best known Asian seaweed stock is called dashi. Dashi is usually made from the seaweed type kombu, dried shiitake mushrooms and dried flakes of tuna which are cooked together. But other seaweed species for example oarweed, vegetables, fish or shrimps can be used to add flavour to the stock. Dashi can be used both as a miso soup and as a base for other soups and sauces. Whether you are serving vegetables or chicken, fish or meat the stock will complement the flavours. It will add umami and thereby intensify the flavour of the other ingredients. To make stock is also a good way of using up leftovers which would otherwise be thrown away, for example vegetable off cuts, roots, and shrimp shells or fish bones. In this book you will find three simple recipes for stock.

DRYING AND STORING

The oldest and best known way of preserving seaweed and kelp is drying. This is the best way to retain the nutrients. When they have dried the volume is reduced by 70–80 percent and they become light to store. As long as the dried seaweed is kept dark and dry it will retain both nutrients and flavour for many years. This is the reason why naturally dried seaweed and kelp are often classified as super-food.

When you have harvested the seaweed you can either hang it up for drying in the sun or dry it in the oven at low temperature (40°C/100°F). To avoid micro organisms causing unwanted smell or taste they should be thoroughly dried for 38 hours. When seaweed is properly dried, it smells salty and fresh – with a touch of liquorice and tobacco. Most of the recipes in this book are made using dried sea vegetables. If you don't want to dry them you can preserve them using other methods. One way is to salt them, the way you salt cod to be used in bacalao. Salted seaweed and kelp can be kept in the fridge for up to six months. Sea vegetables can also be pickled, marinated or frozen.

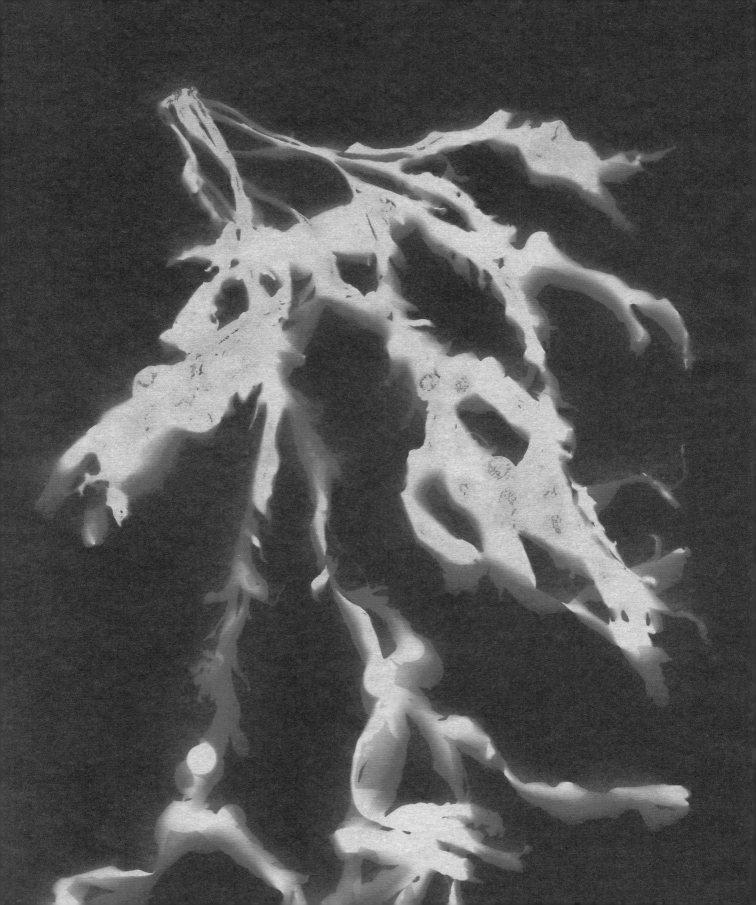

TEXTURE AND FLAVOUR

Vegetables from the sea can be served in many ways: Raw, boiled, baked, grilled, dried or fried, in salads, as a delicious flavour enhancer or as a substitute for salt. Even in small quantities they add good flavours and nutrition. The flavour depends on how the sea vegetables are used; you can procure everything from strong flavours to mildly spicy, sweet and salty. As with the flavour you can produce different textures, depending on the preparation. If the sea vegetables are fried they become lovely and crisp. They go perfectly well as a topping or garnish for soups and stews. If you steam them or serve them fresh, you get an exciting salad with al dente texture. Thus vegetables from the sea are suitable both as a main course and as a garnish for fish and other seafood.

UMAMI

Many modern chefs love sea vegetables not only for their texture and colours. It is also because of the flavour – umami. Maybe you don't know what umami means? That is not so strange because at school we were only taught about four basic flavours: Sweetness, sourness, saltiness and bitterness. This is no longer the case; these days umami is recognised as the fifth flavour.

Umami is a Japanese word from umai (delicious) and mi (essence). The umami taste was identified by Dr. Kikunae Ikeda in 1908. One day when he had the traditional soup, dashi, it tasted exceedingly good. Kelp had intensified the flavour of the soup. Dr. Ikeda made several studies and discovered that the flavourings consisted of the amino acids glutamate and inosinate. They occur naturally in meat, fish, algae and other foods rich in protein. The umami taste could therefore be further refined and used as a flavour enhancer. On its own umami is quite indeterminable and not a dominant taste which is not always easily identifiable, but in combination with other flavours it plays an important role.

NUTRITIONAL CONTENT

Sea vegetables have great nutritional value and offer many health benefits. Anyone who suffers from gluten allergy or follows a low carb diet can benefit from food containing seaweed and kelp. Sea vegetables have few calories, few carbohydrates, and a low fat content. But they are generally protein rich and often contain valuable minerals such as calcium, magnesium and potassium. Many seaweed and kelp species also contain important amino acids and trace elements (such as iron, zinc and selenium) and important vitamins (such as A, B, C, D and E). Some sea vegetables, for example oarweed are also an important source of iodine.

OARWEED

Laminaria Digitata

Oarweed is a tough, leathery brown algae which grows up to three metres long. The species is common all along the coast line and can form dense underwater forests. It is harvested from January to July. Dried oarweed has a lovely, full-bodied sea aroma. It contains mannitol, a naturally occurring sugar molecule which gives the seaweed/kelp a slightly sweet taste, and glutamic acid which is the source for the much coveted umami flavour.

NUTRIENTS
Oarweed is fat free and cholesterol free, rich in food fibres and soluble fibres, iodine, magnesium, potassium and calcium. It also contains rich quantities of Vitamin B.

PREPARATION
Dried oarweed should be soaked in cold water for 15–30 minutes and then left to simmer for 40 minutes. You can also mix in the sea vegetables directly with beans or add them to stock and otherwise follow the instructions in the recipe.

COOKING WITH DRIED OARWEED
Oarweed is indispensible in soups and various types of stock. You can add a leaf of oarweed to anything that needs a little bouillon-like flavour. Oarweed can also be fried, grilled, pickled, boiled, sautéed and marinated. Never boil beans without it, since the oarweed tenderises the beans, reduces the cooking time and makes them easier to digest.

COOKING WITH FRESH OARWEED
Fresh oarweed can be steamed or blanched for 3–5 minutes. It then acquires a verdigris green colour and looks attractive. Boiled oarweed can be finely cut and used in fish soup and fish cakes or as an ingredient in for example coleslaw or in a salad.

· oarweed – laminaria digitata ·

Lamina (lat.) = plate/blade; digitata = finger like.

● MISO SOUP

Serves 4 / 30 minutes

10 g oarweed
1 litre vegetable stock (see recipe on page 81)
1 carrot, cut into fine strips
5 tbsp miso paste
1 spring onion, thinly sliced
4 shiitakes, thinly sliced
Seaweed garnish of laver

Soak the oarweed in cold water for 10 minutes,
rinse and cut into bite-size pieces. Bring the vegetable stock
and oarweed to boil and let it simmer for 10 minutes.
Add the carrot and let it simmer
for approx. 3 minutes.

Turn the miso paste to a bowl and dissolve it in a little of the
vegetable stock before mixing it in with the soup.
Serve in 4 soup bowls and garnish with spring onion.
Slice the mushrooms and laver and add before serving.

Miso soup can be made with all kinds of green vegetables,
for example spinach, green peas or green cabbage.
Tofu cut into small cubes is also delicious in miso soup.

SEA LETTUCE

Ulva Lactuca

Sea lettuce is a verdigris green leaf with a characteristic taste and aroma. It is the most lettuce-like vegetable among the sea vegetables. It is harvested and eaten all over the world and common in temperate and cold waters.

NUTRIENTS

Sea lettuce is rich in protein and contains considerable amounts of food fibres. It is known for its high content of iron and magnesium, as well as high levels of vitamin C and B12.

PREPARATION

This sea vegetable is delicious raw. It has a fresh taste and crisp texture. In dried form it is suitable for use in dressings, pesto and as a flavour enhancing garnish to your favourite dishes. For any other uses follow the instructions in the recipes.

DRIED SEA LETTUCE IN COOKING

Dried sea lettuce is often used as a spice for fish dishes or as an ingredient in, for example, pesto together with fresh herbs.

FRESH SEA LETTUCE IN COOKING

Fresh sea lettuce is delicious in soups or salads and as an accompaniment to fish and other seafood. The clear and beautiful green colour makes it the chef's favourite in the summer, when it can be harvested along the whole coast. Try to add a good quality olive oil, fresh herbs and a little lime or apple cider vinegar.

· sea lettuce – ulva lactuca ·

Ulva is an old plant name, in old Latin used about sea plants; lactuca = salad.

● OMELETTE WITH PEAS, FETA CHEESE AND SEA LETTUCE

Serves 4 / 45 minutes

20 g sea lettuce leaves, coarsely chopped
8 eggs
150 ml milk
2 tsp orange and pistachio spice (see recipe on page 55)
1 tsp seaweed salt
200 g frozen peas, de-frosted
200 g feta cheese, coarsely crumbled
100 g carrot, cut into thin slices
1 spring onion, cut into thin strips
30 g butter
1 tbsp sea lettuce flakes

Preheat the oven to 180°C/350°F/gas 4.
Soak the sea lettuce in water for 10 minutes, then
rinse and drain.
Whisk the eggs and milk.
Add spices, salt, peas, feta cheese, carrot,
spring onion and sea lettuce.

Melt the butter in a large ovenproof frying pan.
Pour the egg mixture into the pan. Bake it in the oven for
30 minutes until the omelette has set and turned golden.
Serve the omelette immediately and sprinkle
a few sea lettuce flakes on top.

WINGED KELP

Alaria Esculenta

Alaria Esculenta means edible wings. It is a hardy feather-like kelp which prefers cool water with many waves and is common along the coast. It has an oblong, dark brown frond and consists of a prominent midrib with a wavy membranous lamina which grows up to 20 cm wide and several metres long. It has a distinctive flavour but still delicate and is the best sea vegetable for salads and a number of other dishes.

NUTRIENTS
Winged kelp is fat free, cholesterol free, rich in vitamin B and C and important minerals such as calcium, iron, magnesium and potassium, as well as enzymes, trace elements and food fibres.

PREPARATION
Soak the kelp/seaweed in cold water for 15-30 minutes. Boil until tender, 5-15 minutes depending on the size.

DRIED WINGED KELP IN COOKING
Winged kelp has a mild taste profile which makes it ideal with many other ingredients without undermining their original flavour. It can be blanched or steamed and used in salads, stews, wok dishes and soups and can be simmered with fish or added to a spicy filling. It tastes especially delicious marinated in lemon and soy sauce as an accompaniment to fish and other seafood, light meat and vegetables.

FRESH WINGED KELP IN COOKING
Winged kelp also becomes a vivid green colour when placed in boiling water. You can use the fresh kelp/seaweed in the same way as the dried one. Take care that you do not boil the winged kelp for too long. It is important that it stays al dente!

· butare – alaria esculenta ·

Ala (lat.) = wing; esculenta = edible. «Edible wings». Other name: Winged kelp.

SALMON WITH COFFEE, CHILLI AND WINGED KELP

Serves 4 / 25 minutes

1½ tsp finely ground coffee
1 tsp coconut sugar (or brown sugar)
1 tsp ground cumin
1 tsp ground coriander seeds
½ tsp chilli flakes
1 tsp salt flakes
½ tsp freshly ground pepper
6 g crushed winged kelp
3 tbsp olive oil

800 g salmon fillet (organic), cut into 4 pieces
1 tbsp olive oil
1 lemon sliced
60 g spring onion, cut lengthwise

½ tsp toasted white sesame seeds
½ tsp toasted black sesame seeds
Fresh coriander

Thoroughly mix all the ingredients for the spice paste and rub the paste
all over the fish. Warm a frying pan over medium heat, pour in the olive oil
and fry the fish fillets in the pan with the skin side down until the skin is crisp.
Turn the fillets over and fry them on the other side until golden.
Remove from the pan and set aside to rest.
Fry the spring onion lightly in the pan and arrange it with the
lemon slices on four plates. Finally place the salmon on top.
Decorate with toasted sesame seeds and fresh coriander.

THONGWEED/SEA SPAGHETTI

Himanthalia Elongata

Thongweed is also known as sea spaghetti. It is found in inlets in exposed areas. At the base the plant resembles small button-like discs, either flat or saucer-shaped (up to 3 cm in diameter) which are attached to the base with a short stalk. Long thongs (the reproductive organs) grow from the discs. In the autumn the thongs decay and only the discs remain. The seaweed can be harvested from early spring until summer, when the colour is light green and fresh.

NUTRIENTS
Thongweed has a good balance of minerals, vitamins and trace elements. It is a rich source of magnesium, calcium and iron.

PREPARATION
Soak the thongweed in cold water for approx. 15 minutes. Rinse and discard the water. It is now ready for boiling or marinating. Cooking time is approx. 5–15 minutes, depending on the size. For other ideas follow the instructions in the recipe.

DRIED THONGWEED/SEA SPAGHETTI IN COOKING
Thongweed has a nutlike flavour and is delicious in pasta dishes as well as in meat – and vegetables stews. It goes well with tomatoes and can be marinated or pickled. When it is dried and pulverised, it can for example be added to a grill sauce. It also works well with both meat and fish and goes surprisingly well with liquorice powder.

FRESH THONGWEED/SEA SPAGHETTI IN COOKING
Thongweed is lovely when it is fresh. It is crisp and mild. You can use the fresh seaweed as a vegetable in salads, pasta and soups.

· thongweed / sea spaghetti – himanthalia elongata ·

(Linnaeus) is a brown alga (Phaeophyceae).

● PASTA WITH THONGWEED AND GRILLED TOMATOES

Serves 4 / 45 minutes

20 g dried thongweed
750 g cherry tomatoes, cut in half
1 tsp thyme dried or fresh
2 garlic cloves sliced
Seaweed salt
Pepper
2 tbsp olive oil
500 g spaghetti
1 tsp mixed seaweed flakes
1 handful fresh basil

Soak the dried thongweed in cold water while you prepare
the other ingredients. Preheat the oven to 200°C/400°F/gas 6.
Place the tomatoes in an oven tray and sprinkle with
herbs, garlic and seaweed salt.
Bake in the oven for 20 minutes. Use half of the tomatoes
for decoration and put the rest through a blender for
approx. 1 minute.
Season the tomato sauce with seaweed salt and pepper.

Boil the spaghetti and thongweed for 10 minutes
in separate pots. Arrange the spaghetti, thongweed,
tomato sauce and grilled tomatoes in soup plates.
Sprinkle with seaweed and decorate with basil.

DULSE

Palmaria Palmata

Dulse is a soft and beautiful, little leathery red alga which grows on rocks, other seaweed and kelp plants at low water levels and down to 30 metres along many coastlines. The flat fronds are often forked in broad segments and new fronds can grow out at the edge of the frond. The alga can grow up to 50 cm long, but is generally 10-20 cm. Dulse has a characteristic flavour and a deep red colour.
It is a colourful salad ingredient, tastes delicious in soups, achieves a piquant flavour when fried, and enhances the flavour in any sandwich.

NUTRIENTS
Dulse is an excellent source of iodine. It contains a good deal of protein compared with vegetables grown on land. It is rich in iron, calcium and magnesium and is a good source of vitamin B and C.

PREPARATION
Dried dulse does not need to be soaked or cooked, so it can be enjoyed as a delicious snack directly from the bag or added as a flavour enhancer to hot dishes just before serving.

DRIED DULSE IN COOKING
Dulse can be used in a number of different dishes. The characteristic smoked flavour makes it an ideal companion to potatoes, soup, green cabbage, eggs and cheese. Dulse is a piquant and unusual companion for chocolate as well as a fantastic ingredient in ice cream, puddings and toffee.

FRESH DULSE IN COOKING
Fresh dulse tastes completely different from dried, fermented dulse and has completely different uses. A favourite is pesto, tartar or quite simply fried in butter in the frying pan with a little lemon juice squeezed over.

· dulse – palmaria palmata ·

Palmaria palmata. Palma (lat.) = palm; palmata = hand shaped.

● SALT-BAKED POTATOES
WITH DULSE

Serves 4 / 45 minutes

800 g small potatoes, peeled and cut in half
3 tbsp olive oil
3 garlic cloves, sliced
1 tsp salt flakes
10 g dulse
2 tsp dulse flakes

Preheat the oven to 200°C/400°F/gas 6.
Mix the potatoes with olive oil, garlic and salt
flakes and put them on an oven tray with a grid.
Bake for 30 minutes.
Five minutes before the end
of the cooking time sprinkle with whole
dulse leaves and dulse flakes.

LAVER

Porphyra Umbilicali

Laver is a lovely scarlet sea vegetable which grows on stony beaches from early spring until late into autumn. It has a smooth structure and forms large thin fronds which you will often find glued to stones on the shoreline at low tide. The iodine content gives this sea vegetable a characteristic flavour which is a bit like olives and oysters. When frying laver in a frying pan it takes on a bacon-like nutty flavour.

NUTRIENTS
In terms of nutrients laver has the highest content of vitamin B1, B6, B12, C and E of all the sea vegetables included in this book. It also contains considerable amounts of vegetable proteins, fibres, and several minerals, especially iron and trace elements.

PREPARATION
Laver can be eaten raw, cooked or dried. Before cooking the laver should be rinsed several times in clean water to remove any sand. To get the nutty, sweet flavour you can fry the laver lightly in a frying pan or at low temperature in the oven until it acquires the slightly green colour. Follow the instructions in the recipes.

DRIED LAVER IN COOKING
Dried laver can be crumbled and sprinkled over soups, salads, pasta, eggs, potatoes or any dish which needs a hint of the flavour of the sea. Laver is also delicious in cakes, bread and granola.

FRESH LAVER IN COOKING
In Europe the use of laver is best known from the traditional Welsh laver bread, where the laver is cooked for many hours before mixing it with bacon and oats. Fresh laver has a lovely delicate flavour and can be used in salads or otherwise steamed as a vegetable.

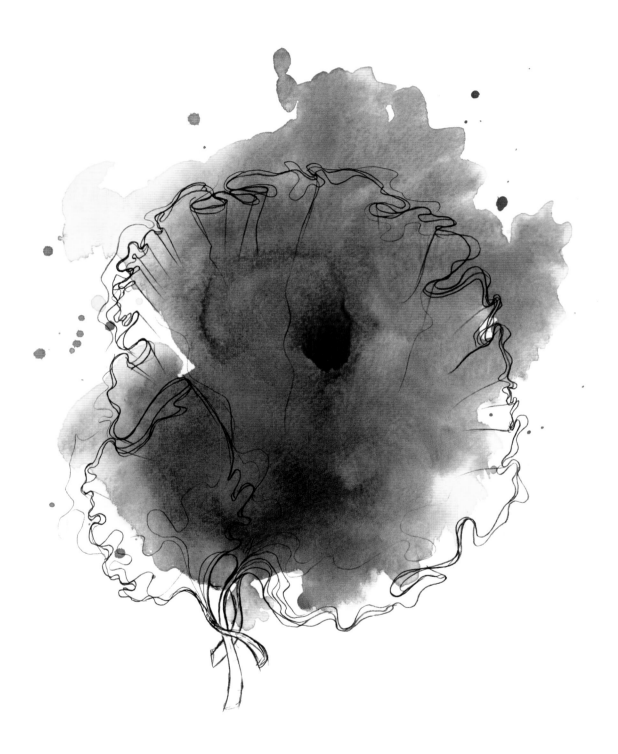

· laver – porphyra umbilicali ·

Porphyra (gr.) = scarlet (like the colour from scarlet snail); umbilicalis = with navel (as the plant as an attachment in the middle).

TOAST WITH TOMATO AND LAVER

Serves 4 / 25 minutes

4 slices sourdough bread
20 g whole laver leaves
1 clove garlic, cut in half
4 tomatoes, 2 cut in half and 2 thinly sliced
4 tbsp olive oil
2 tsp seaweed salt

Preheat the oven to 200°C/400°F/gas 6.
Place the slices of bread and the laver leaves on baking
paper and bake in the oven for 3 minutes until golden and crisp.
Remove from the oven and immediately rub both sides
of the bread with the cut side of the half garlic clove.

Then rub the same side of the bread slices with the cut side of
half a tomato and squeeze a little of the fruit pulp onto the sliced
bread. Drizzle a little olive oil over and cover the bread slices with
slices of tomato and crisp laver leaves.

Sprinkle a little seaweed salt on top.
Serve the bread slices while still hot and crisp.

SEABELT

Saccharina Latissima

Seabelt is found in the north-east Atlantic Ocean and the Barents Sea south to Galicia in Spain. It is common round the coasts of the British Isles. It is harvested in early spring when the water is ice cold and clear. Seabelt is yellow brown with a long, narrow undivided blade which can grow up to 3 metres long and 50 centimetres wide. The central band is dimpled like the skin of an alligator, while the margin is smooth with wavy edges. Seabelt is rich in umami and is well suited as a salt substitute and flavour enhancer in cooking.

NUTRIENTS
Seabelt is fat free and cholesterol free, rich in food fibres and soluble fibres, iodine, magnesium, potassium and calcium.

PREPARATION
Dried seabelt does generally not have to be soaked. The fine leaves can be crushed and used for sprinkling.

DRIED SEABELT IN COOKING
Seabelt is especially suitable as a spice for soups, stews, sauces and vegetarian dishes. Seabelt also tastes delicious fried with nuts and seeds and can be added to granola or sprinkled over a chocolate cake. Seabelt contains a lot of alginate and can be used as a thickening agent.

FRESH SEABELT IN COOKING
Seabelt can be tied round fish and chicken to be oven baked or steamed. When the seabelt is quite young the fine leaves can be tied round seafood as an ingredient in tapas or sushi.

· seabelt – saccharina latissima ·

Saccharina = sugar like; latissima = broad/very wide,cf. The size of the leaves. (Until 2006 it was known as Laminaria saccharina).

● BAKED CARROTS WITH SEABELT, HONEY, CHILLI AND SOYA

Serves 4 / 45 minutes

8 carrots, peeled and cut in half lengthwise
1 tbsp honey
2 dried chillies or 1 tsp chilli flakes
4 tbsp soy sauce
2 tbsp olive oil
2 tsp ground cumin
3 garlic cloves sliced
1 pinch seaweed salt
1 tbsp seabelt flakes
Fresh thyme

Preheat the oven to 200°C/400°F/gas 6.
Place the carrots cut in half in an ovenproof dish.
Mix honey, chilli, soy sauce, olive oil, cumin,
garlic and place in a small bowl.
Spread the mixture over the carrots. Sprinkle with
seabelt flakes. Put the carrots in the oven
and cook for 30 minutes.
Turn on the grill for the last 5-10 minutes.
Sprinkle with a little fresh thyme just
before serving.

SEAWEED SALT

We are using too much salt in our food. A clever way of reducing salt consumption is to make your own seaweed salt. In this way you will also include an extra supplement of minerals and vitamins in your food. It is very easy to make your own seaweed salt. You can mix your favourite salt flakes with one or several types of flakes or granules of seaweed and kelp.

Any combination of dulse, laver and seabelt are suitable for mixing with salt.

● SEAWEED SALT WITH SEABELT

Mix 50 % salt flakes with 50 % seabelt flakes.

●● MIXED SEAWEED SALT

Mix 60 % salt flakes with 20 % sprinkle of dulse and 20 % sprinkle of laver.

●● ORANGE AND PISTACHIO SPICE

25 minutes

30 g pistachio nuts
5 g dulse
15 g white sesame seeds
¼ orange zest (organic)
10 g seabelt flakes
1 pinch cumin
1 pinch chilli powder
1 pinch sea salt

Preheat the oven to 150°C/300°F/gas 2 and cook the pistachio nuts, dulse, sesame seeds and orange zest on a baking tray for approx. 10 minutes. Then mix all the ingredients and grind them in a mortar or blend them carefully in a food processor (use the pulse button).

● SEAWEED ZAATAR

15 minutes

5 g dried thyme
30 g toasted sesame seeds
10 g dulse flakes
2 tsp sumac
Zest of ½ lemon, organic

Preheat the oven to 150°C/300°F/gas 2 and roast all the ingredients on a baking tray for approx. 10 minutes. Then mix all the ingredients well and grind in a mortar.

●● SEAWEED DUKKAH

20 minutes

50 g hazelnuts
30 g sesame seeds
10 g dried seabelt
5 g dried laver
5 g coriander
5 g cumin
5 g salt flakes
5 g black pepper

Preheat the oven to 150°C/300°F/gas 2. Place all the ingredients on a baking sheet and roast for approx. 10 minutes. Mix them well and grind the mixture in a mortar.

●● HOME-MADE FURIKAKE
50 minutes

1 orange (organic)
30 g white sesame seeds
30 g black sesame seeds
5 g sprinkle dulse
5 g sprinkle laver
½ tsp salt
½ tsp chilli powder or chilli flakes

Preheat the oven to 110°C/225°F/gas ¼. Peel the orange thinly with a potato peeler, cut the yellow peel into coarse pieces, place in an oven dish and roast the peel for approx. 30 minutes until dry. Grind the peel in a mortar or carefully blend in a food mixer. Use the pulse button. Toast the sesame seeds in a frying pan. Mix all the ingredients and keep the furikake in an airtight box.

SUN-DRIED TOMATO DIP

Serves 4 / 20 minutes

---

5 g dulse
100 g sun-dried tomatoes
1 roasted red pepper
50 g blanched almonds
½ shallot
½ clove garlic
40 ml olive oil
½ tsp white balsamic vinegar
1 tbsp maple syrup
1 tsp smoked paprika
Salt
Pepper

Preheat the oven to 200°C/400°F/gas 6 and roast
3 g dulse for 5 minutes. Mix 2 g dulse, sun-dried
tomatoes, pepper, almonds, shallot, garlic, olive oil,
balsamic vinegar, maple syrup, smoked paprika, salt
and pepper to a coarse mixture and decorate the dip
with the dulse roasted to a crisp.

PARSLEY PESTO

Serves 4 / 15 minutes

---

8 g dried winged kelp
50 g parsley, coarsely chopped
50 g walnuts, coarsley chopped
25 g pecorino (or Parmesan), freshly grated
2 tsp lime juice
Zest of lime (organic)
2 g fresh ginger root, peeled and chopped
½ garlic clove, peeled and chopped
50 ml olive oil
6 g sea salt
Pepper

Soak the winged kelp for 30 minutes in water, then
drain and squeeze out the water. Chop coarsely.
Combine all the ingredients to a coarse mixture.

CELERIAC DIP

Serves 4 / 15 minutes

---

200 g cooked celeriac
30 g hazelnuts, roasted, the brown skin removed
2 tsp sesame seed oil
1 tsp white rice vinegar
½ tsp salt
1 pinch of pepper
1 tbsp fresh coriander, coarsely chopped
   (for decoration)
1 tbsp seabelt flakes

Mix celeriac, hazelnuts, sesame seed oil, rice vinegar,
salt and pepper to a coarse mixture. Serve the dip
decorated with coriander and flakes of seabelt.

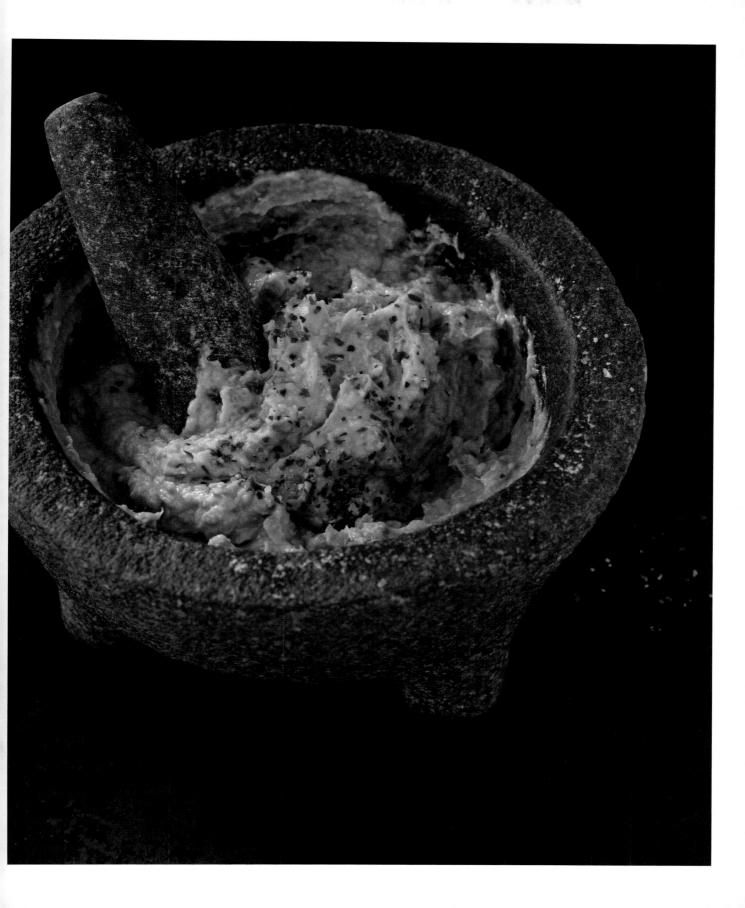

GUACAMOLE

Serves 8 / 15 minutes

4 ripe avocados
Juice of 3 limes
1 small white onion, finely chopped
¼ tsp ground black pepper
1 tsp seaweed salt
2 garlic cloves, finely chopped
1 chilli, finely chopped
2 tsp dulse flakes

Mash the avocado flesh with a fork in a bowl. Mix in immediately the rest of the ingredients and serve the guacamole straight away.

PUMPKIN DIP

Serves 4 / 15 minutes

450 g roasted pumpkin
35 g cream cheese
30 g walnuts
1 tsp olive oil
1 tbsp maple syrup
1 g grated fresh ginger
Pinch of sea salt
1 tsp maple syrup
Pinch of chilli flakes
2 g roasted chopped thongweed

Blend all the ingredients to a coarse paste in a food processor. Serve the dip garnished with chilli flakes and chopped thongweed.

HUMMUS

Serves 4 / 15 minutes

4 g seabelt (topping)
1 tsp sweet paprika (topping)
1 tin cooked chickpeas (total weight 265 g)
1 garlic clove
1 tsp lemon juice
Zest of 1 lime
2 tbsp tahini
2 tbsp olive oil
2 tsp balsamic vinegar
½ tsp toasted cumin
½ tsp freshly chopped rosemary
Salt
Cayenne pepper

Preheat the oven to 200°C/400°F/gas 6 and toast the seabelt and paprika for 5 minutes. Put all the other ingredients in a food processor and blend to a coarse mixture. Serve the hummus garnished with a mixture of roasted seabelt and roasted paprika.

FERMENTING

It is easy, fun and healthy to make your own fermented vegetables. Seaweed works well with beetroot, green cabbage and other cabbage. You can use all types of dried or fresh seaweed. In the following we give you a very simple recipe for fermented cabbage with seaweed. We suggest that you read about fermenting to gain more information, good advice and inspiration.

● FERMENTED CABBAGE WITH SEAWEED
45 minutes

2 kg cabbage, finely cut
1 level tbsp unrefined sea salt
1 tbsp caraway seeds
30 g winged kelp, soaked for approx. 30 minutes

Put the cabbage in a large bowl and sprinkle with salt and caraway seeds. Press down the cabbage, so the salt draws the water out from the cabbage. This forms the brine in which the cabbage ferments without rotting. The salt also makes sure that the cabbage will keep crisp by preventing organisms and enzymes, which make the cabbage soft.

Place cabbage and seaweed in layers in a large pickling jar or crock. With each handful of cabbage, you press it down, to ensure that the brine covers the vegetables. If you do not have enough brine, make a little extra by dissolving salt in water. The brine should taste good and not be too salty.

To ensure that the brine covers the vegetables all the time, you can place a small pickling jar filled with water as a weight on top, or place a zip lock bag filled with brine on top of the vegetables.
When the vegetables are covered with brine leave the glass or crock at room temperature so the cabbage can ferment. Cover the opening with a small towel. After a few days the cabbage starts to ferment and develops a good, sour taste.

When you think it is sour enough you can start eating from it and keep it in a cool place.

Fermenting: 10–20 days at room temperature.

COCOA AND CHIPOTLE MARINADE
10 minutes

1 tbsp dark cocoa powder
2 tsp Tabasco chipotle sauce
1 tsp dried oregano
2 tsp smoked paprika
2 tbsp red wine vinegar
1 tsp finely chopped garlic
1 tbsp olive oil
3 tbsp canola oil
1 tbsp maple syrup
4 g dulse

Blend everything together in a food processor. This marinade is quite dark and full bodied with a smoky taste, so it goes well with roasted vegetables, salmon, game or tofu.

SWEET CHILLI AND LAVER MARINADE
10 minutes

2 tsp fresh red chilli, chopped
2 tsp chilli paste
4 tbsp finely chopped red pepper
1 tbsp soy sauce
4 tbsp sesame seed oil
2 tsp lime juice
2 tbsp honey
4 g flakes laver or nori

Blend all the ingredients in a food processor. The chilli marinade is sharp, sweet and spicy. It goes well with pasta, sautéed vegetables, grilled chicken or pork, shrimps or Asian soups.

● SEA LETTUCE MARINADE
10 minutes

2 g sea lettuce, chopped
2 g mint leaves, chopped
100 g green tomatoes, chopped
4 g lime zest (organic)
2 tsp chopped lemon grass
2 tbsp lemon juice
1 tbsp extra virgin olive oil
3 tbsp grape seed oil
2 tsp green Tabasco sauce

Blend all the ingredients in a food processor. The sea lettuce marinade is quite mild and sour and goes well with white fish, lobster and vegetables.

● BBQ SAUCE WITH SEAWEED
45 minutes

400 g tin skinless, chopped tomatoes
2 pieces oarweed
5 tbsp brown sugar
4 tbsp honey
1 tsp smoked paprika
1 tsp chipotle
100 ml red wine vinegar
½ tsp coriander seeds
1 onion, chopped

Mix all the ingredients and cook them for 30 minutes over open fire. Then blend everything in a food processor and leave the sauce to cool. This sauce goes well with all kinds of grilled food.

●● ASPARAGUS WITH GORGONZOLA SAUCE

Serves 4 / 45 minutes

ASPARAGUS

1 piece oarweed
1 pinch of sea salt
½ orange (organic)
500 g green asparagus, peeled,
    break off the lower woody stem
500 g white asparagus, peeled,
    break off the lower woody stem
Iced water

Place the oarweed in boiling water with a little sea
salt. Squeeze the orange and pour in the orange juice
mixed with the orange pulp. Cook the asparagus until
tender. Leave the asparagus to cool in the iced water,
drain well and set aside.

GORGONZOLA SAUCE

2 soft boiled eggs
2 tsp white wine vinegar
2 tbsp soft butter
6 tbsp cold vegetable stock (see recipe page 81)
6 tbsp vegetable oil
100 g mild blue cheese

Blend the soft boiled eggs with vinegar and butter in a
food processor. Without stopping the machine add
the stock a spoon at a time and add the oil in a thin
drizzle, so the liquids will be well mixed. Finally add
the blue cheese.
Leave the sauce at room temperature.

TOPPING

50 g toasted hazelnuts
4 g dulse
4 g orange zest (organic)
10 g strong blue cheese, crumbled
Fresh cress

Arrange the asparagus evenly on four plates. Pour
over the sauce. Finally sprinkle the topping over the
sauce and over the asparagus.

● SEABELT BREAD AND CELERIAC DIP

2 slices of bread / 2 hours

---

20 g fresh yeast
½ tbsp sugar
200 ml water
2 tbsp cumin seeds
400 g barley flour
350 g coarse wholemeal spelt
1½ tbsp salt
20 g seabelt flakes

Mix yeast and sugar with hand-hot water. Leave on one side for 10 minutes in a warm place. Toast the cumin seeds in a frying pan and then grind them in a mortar. Mix barley flour, spelt flour, salt and the yeast mixture to a soft dough in a medium-sized bowl. Add the cumin and the seabelt flakes. Knead the dough thoroughly. Divide the dough into two equal pieces and shape into bread. Leave to rest in a warm place for approx. one hour. Using a sharp knife quickly score the surface of the loaves. Slash each at a 45-degree angle 4 to 5 times along the loaf's axis.

Preheat the oven to 220°C/425°F/gas 7. Cook the breads in the oven for 30 minutes. During the cooking sprinkle the loaves several times with a little cold water to get a crisp crust.

Serve the bread with celeriac dip (see recipe page 61).

STOCK

Seaweed is an excellent ingredient for all kinds of soups. To get a good flavour in the soup, it is a good idea to make a stock first. You will need a few pieces of dried oarweed, a few vegetables, for example leek, onion, carrots, celery, mushrooms or other vegetables you may have to hand, as well as a few herbs such as parsley, lovage , bay leaf, thyme or any other fresh or dried herb.

Food which would otherwise go to waste can be used for making stock. It could be the green part of root vegetables, shells and shrimp shells and off-cuts from fish and bones – everything contributes to giving the stock a lovely flavour.

● FISH STOCK
30 minutes

1 litre water
3 carrots, sliced
2 onions, sliced
3 celery stalks, chopped
1 small bunch parsley (you can also use the stalks)
Off-cuts from white fish such as cod,
    haddock or pollock
3 pieces dried oarweed (15 g)
100 ml white wine
1 tsp coriander
1 tsp whole black pepper

Bring the water to the boil. Add all the ingredients and leave to simmer for 20 minutes. Then pour the stock through a sieve. Use the stock you need and put the rest in the freezer so you have ready-made stock for the next time.

VEGETABLE STOCK
1 hour

2 leeks, only the green parts, coarsely chopped
1 onion, sliced
1 garlic clove, chopped
1 carrot, sliced
¼ celeriac, coarsely chopped
A few pieces of oarweed (15 g)
10 black peppercorns
1 bay leaf
1 small bunch of parsley (you can also use the stalks)

Place all the vegetables in a large saucepan. Pour cold water over the vegetables so the water level is approx. 5 cm over the vegetables. Bring to the boil and leave to simmer over low heat for approx. 40 minutes. Leave to cool before sieving the stock. You can use the stock for soup or keep in the fridge for up to 5 days or it can be frozen.

You can also use seaweed in meat stock. Seaweed gives the stock a delicate, slightly thicker consistency and enhances the flavour of all the other ingredients.

MUSHROOM STOCK
1 hour 30 minutes

1 onion, thinly sliced
1 leek, only the green part, washed and chopped
4 garlic cloves, with the skin on, crushed with the flat end of a knife
30 g dried boletus mushrooms
2 carrots, chopped
3 pieces of dried oarweed (15 g)
6 parsley stalks, coarsely chopped
2 oregano stalks
2 litres cold water

Place the onion, leek, garlic, mushrooms, carrots, oarweed, parsley and oregano in a large saucepan. Add the water and bring to the boil. Leave to simmer without a lid for 1 hour. Sieve the stock and squeeze as much stock as possible out of the vegetables before discarding.

● FISH SOUP

Serves 4 / 35 minutes

10 g thongweed
6 shallots, sliced
1 red pepper, cut into cubes
2 skinless tomatoes, sliced
2 tbsp paprika
½ chilli, chopped
4 garlic cloves, chopped
1 tbsp olive oil
1 litre fish stock (see recipe page 80)
100 ml white wine
2 stalks oregano
400 g mussels
500 g fish fillet, cut into chunks
2–3 tbsp lime juice

Place the thongweed in water to soak. Fry the
shallots, pepper, tomatoes, paprika, chilli and garlic in
the oil.
Add the fish stock, white wine and oregano and cook
for 20 minutes. Cut the thongweed into suitable
pieces and leave it to cook with the soup for the last
10 minutes.
Add mussels and fish fillet and heat until mussels
open and fish is cooked. Squeeze a little lime juice
over at the end.

● RAMEN

Serves 4 / 30 minutes

---

1 pack Asian soup noodles
1 litre vegetable stock (see recipe page 81)
2 tbsp soy sauce
1 tbsp lime juice
4 cm fresh ginger, grated
1 stalk lemon grass, chopped
2 garlic cloves, chopped
½ fresh, red chilli, chopped
10 g laver
4 tbsp light miso
4 egg yolks
Fresh dill or fresh coriander, chopped
1 spring onion, chopped
Handful of small spinach leaves
50 g enoki mushrooms

Cook the noodles for 5 minutes. Put aside. Boil the
stock with soy sauce, lime juice, ginger, lemon grass,
laver, garlic and chilli. Add the miso paste. Pour the
egg yolks and the noodles into the warm soup. Serve
the dish warm. Sprinkle herbs, spinach, spring onions
and enoki mushrooms on top.

ICE COOL CUCUMBER AND MELON GAZPACHO

Serves 4 / 1 hour and 30 minutes

5 g winged kelp, soaked in water
¼ slice day-old bread, the crust cut away
200 g cucumber, (150 g peeled and coarsely
   chopped, 50 g finely chopped)
1 red pepper, seeds removed, (½ coarsely chopped,
   ½ finely chopped)
2 garlic cloves
300 g watermelon, peeled and the seeds removed,
   (50 g finely chopped, the remainder coarsely
   chopped)
3 ripe tomatoes, sliced
150 g fish fillet (cod) in fine cubes, blanched

TOPPING
3 tbsp extra virgin olive oil
1 tbsp agave syrup
3 tbsp lemon juice
1 small chilli, finely chopped
Seaweed salt, freshly ground black pepper

Cook the winged kelp for 10 minutes, rinse under
cold water and chop. Set aside. Soak the bread with
100 ml water for 15 minutes. Blend coarsely chopped
cucumber, coarsely chopped pepper, garlic, coarsely
chopped watermelon and tomatoes in a food
processor for 30 seconds. Add the softened bread, 2
tbsp olive oil, 1 tbsp agave syrup and 1 tbsp lemon
juice. Blend all the ingredients for 1 minute. Season
the soup to taste with seaweed salt and pepper. Pour
the soup into a pitcher and place in the freezer and
freeze for 30 minutes.

Then add chilli, fish fillet, finely chopped pepper,
melon and cucumber. Leave the mixture for the
flavours to develop for 10 minutes. To make the
topping mix 1 tbsp olive oil, 2 tbsp lemon juice,
chopped winged kelp and sea salt. Serve the gazpacho
ice cold with topping.

MARINATED FISH WITH DULSE AND GRAPEFRUIT

Serves 4 / 30 minutes

MARINADE
1 tbsp lime juice
2 tbsp grapefruit juice
½ tsp fresh, peeled ginger
1 tsp fresh coriander, chopped
1 tbsp olive oil

300 g fish fillet (cod), thinly sliced
½ tsp grapefruit zest, finely grated (organic, only
   the yellow part)
2 tsp dulse flakes
Salt flakes
Freshly ground pepper

TOPPING
½ grapefruit, peeled and thinly sliced
Fresh cress
4 slices coarse crisp bread

Mix lime juice, grapefruit juice, ginger, coriander and
olive oil. Place the fish and the grapefruit zest in a box
with a close-fitting lid, pour over the marinade and
leave the mixture for 15 minutes. Season the fish with
dulse flakes, salt flakes and freshly ground pepper.
Arrange the grapefruit slices and the fish on four
plates and decorate with fresh cress. Serve with coarse
crisp bread.

Use whole fresh fish for this dish. If you place the fish
fillet in the freezer for 20 minutes, it is easier to cut
the fish into thin slices.

● VEGETARIAN SPRING ROLLS
Serves 4 / 45 minutes

SAUCE FOR DIPPING
100 ml water
100 ml soy sauce
1 tbsp mirin
50 g brown sugar
½ chopped garlic
1 red chilli, thinly sliced into rings
2 tsp dulse flakes
1 tbsp lime juice

Heat the water, soy sauce, mirin, brown sugar, garlic, chilli and 1 tsp dulse flakes in a small saucepan over medium heat and stir until everything is thoroughly mixed. Bring the mixture to the boil and leave to simmer for 6-8 minutes. Remove the saucepan from the heat, cool the mixture and add the lime juice.

SPRING ROLLS
8 round sheets of rice paper
3 carrots, peeled and thinly sliced lengthwise
100 g fresh greens, e.g. rocket or pea shoots
½ cucumber, cut into long thin slices
1 avocado, peeled and the stone removed, the flesh finely chopped and mixed with 1 tbsp lime juice
1 tbsp furikake (see recipe page 56)

Place the rice papers to soften in cold water for 2 minutes. Place them one at a time on a chopping board and place carrots, greens, cucumber, and avocado in a stripe in the middle of the rice paper. Sprinkle a little furikake and 1 tsp dulse flakes on top. Fold over the short ends and roll the rice paper into a parcel. Cut each roll in half and serve with the dipping sauce.

● FREESTYLE SUSHI

Serves 4 / 1hour and 30 minutes (plus 12 hours for marinating)

3 tbsp white rice vinegar
½ tsp salt
1 tbsp sugar
200 g sushi rice
230 ml water

Bring vinegar, salt and sugar to the boil in a small
saucepan until the sugar and salt has dissolved. Rinse
the rice in cold water for 1-2 minutes until clear of
starch. Place the rice in a saucepan and add water.
Bring the rice to the boil, stir now and again and leave
to simmer over low heat for 7-8 minutes. Stir the rice
and leave to rest under a lid for 5 minutes. Place the
rice in a plastic bowl, add the vinegar mixture and
leave to cool.

3 tbsp sesame seeds, black and white mixed
2 tsp chilli flakes
1 tbsp dulse flakes
½ cucumber, cut into cubes
1 avocado, peeled and diced, sprinkled with lemon
40 g whole dulse leaves
100 ml soy sauce
1–2 tsp wasabi

Fry the sesame seeds in a dry frying pan. Then mix
sesame seeds, chilli flakes and 1 tbsp dulse flakes. Make
a ball of rice, place cucumber and avocado in the
middle and close. Roll all the rice balls in the sesame
seed mixture. Then wrap the balls in dulse leaves.

Serve with soy sauce, lemon and ginger pickle
and wasabi.

LEMON AND GINGER PICKLE
200 ml rape seed oil
2 tsp turmeric
200 g ginger, peeled and thinly sliced
2 lemons, thinly sliced
1 tbsp mustard seeds
3 tbsp lemon juice

Heat the oil in a large saucepan. Add turmeric, ginger,
lemon slices and mustard seeds. Leave to simmer for
approx. 20 minutes. Remove the saucepan from the
heat and add the lemon juice. Leave the mixture to
infuse for 24 hours.

●● A SERVING DISH WITH FRUITS OF THE SEA
Serves 4 / 1 hour

SEABELT MAYONNAISE
1 large egg yolk
1 tsp finely grated zest lime (only the green peel)
2 tsp freshly squeezed lime juice
2 tbsp grape seed oil or vegetable oil
1½ tsp green wasabi
1 tsp soy sauce
1 tsp seabelt

Whisk together the egg yolk, grated lime zest and lime juice in a medium-sized bowl. Continue to whisk while slowly adding the oil, a drop at a time to begin with, then whisk the mayonnaise till it thickens and is smooth and even. Season to taste with wasabi, soy sauce and seabelt. Place the mayonnaise in the fridge.

MARINADE
4 g seabelt
4 g fresh ginger, peeled and grated
3 g garlic, crushed
4 g celeriac, grated
2 g jalapeño, finely chopped
Juice of 1 lime
A few drops of toasted sesame seed oil
Pinch of salt
Pinch of white pepper

Mix all the ingredients for the marinade and set aside.

ON THE DISH
3 g thongweed
3 g laver
200 g octopus
230 g squid
320 g fresh cod, raw
8 g trout or salmon caviar
120 g smoked mussels

TOPPING
Petals of marigold
Seaweed salt (see recipe page 53)
Chive flowers
Fennel flowers

Preheat the oven to 180°C/350°F/gas 4 and roast the laver and thongweed for appprox. 5 minutes. Set aside. Sear the octopus and squid in a very hot pan for about 1 minute. Pour the mayonnaise into the middle of the dish and arrange the sea food, fish and the roasted seaweed right across. Pour over the marinade and decorate with flowers, seaweed salt and petals.

●● CELERIAC POTATOES WITH AIOLI AND GREEN SALSA

Serves 4 / 50 minutes

700 g celeriac, peeled and cut into thin strips
500 g potatoes, peeled and cut into thin strips
15 g fine polenta
2 tbsp olive oil
2 tsp salt
2 tsp seabelt flakes

Preheat the oven to 200°C/400°F/gas 6. Mix potatoes, celeriac and polenta, place in an ovenproof dish with olive oil. Mix everything thoroughly and roast the celeriac and potato strips in the oven for 15-20 minutes. Mix salt and seabelt flakes. When the celeriac and potato strips are golden sprinkle the salt mixture over.

AIOLI WITH DULSE
2 egg yolks
½ tsp Dijon mustard
Pinch chopped garlic
½ tsp whole mustard seeds
1 tsp white wine vinegar
200 ml canola oil
1 tsp lemon juice
30 ml olive oil
3–5 g sprinkles of dulse

Mix egg yolks, mustard, garlic, mustard seeds and vinegar to a paste in a blender. Add the canola oil slowly in a thin drizzle while the machine is still running. Without stopping the machine add the lemon juice and the olive oil in a thin drizzle. Finally sprinkle in the dulse.

GREEN SALSA
300 g green tomatoes
50 g pimientos
70 g green pepper
10 g basil
1 tsp lime juice
1 tsp jalapĕno Tabasco
1 garlic clove, chopped
1 tbsp grape seed oil
1 green chilli
1 tsp sea salt
1 tsp sprinkle of laver

Chop tomatoes, pimientos, green pepper and basil. Mix with the rest of the ingredients. Leave to rest for 10 minutes before serving.

● DIM SUM

Serves 4 / 1 hour and 30 minutes

THE DOUGH
250 g rice flour
150 ml water
1 tsp salt

Place two thirds of the flour in a large bowl with the salt and add 150 ml water a little at a time. Knead the dough and add the rest of the flour until the dough is smooth and elastic. Wrap the dough in cling film and leave to rest for one hour. Divide the dough into 12 equal sized portions. Sprinkle flour on a baking tray, place each ball of dough on it and flatten them with your hand. Using a small rolling pin roll each bun to a circle. Roll from the centre and over all of the edges.

PEANUT SAUCE
30 g peanut butter
2 tbsp olive oil
½ chilli chopped
1 tsp rice vinegar
Salt and pepper

Mix all the ingredients for the sauce and set aside.

THE FILLING
40 g quinoa
150 ml water
20 g freshly grated ginger
10 g chopped garlic
200 g spinach, chopped
60 g spring onions, chopped
150 g sprouts, chopped
12 g seabelt, coarsely crushed
25 ml sesame seed oil
20 g tamarind sauce
1 tsp Chinese five spice (star anise, fennel, cinnamon, cloves and Sichuan pepper)
Salt and pepper
Chives

Boil the quinoa in the water until all the liquid has been absorbed. Mix the quinoa with the rest of the ingredients and arrange it equally on the dough. Make sure that you leave a 2 cm wide strip along the edge. Close the parcels by twisting the dough into a knot at the top. Put a large saucepan filled with 2 cm boiling water over strong heat. When the water boils place a sieve over the saucepan, add the dim sum and put a lid on top. Steam the parcels for 15 minutes, or until they are light and airy and cooked through. Tie each parcel with a chive stem and serve immediately with the peanut sauce on the side.

● QUINOA RISOTTO WITH COCKLES

Serves 4 / 40 minutes

200 g quinoa
3 tbsp hazelnut or olive oil
2 shallots, finely chopped
3 garlic cloves, finely chopped
2 small leeks, only the white part finely chopped
150 ml white wine
200 ml fish stock (see recipe page 80)
500 g cockles
6 g laver
70 g Parmesan, finely grated
1 small handful basil, coarsely chopped

Roast the quinoa in a dry saucepan. In another saucepan heat up 3 tbsp oil and fry the shallots, garlic and leeks. Add the quinoa together with white wine and fish stock. Bring to the boil and cook for 10 minutes. Add the cockles and check if they open (2-3 minutes). Preheat the oven to 200°C/400°F/gas 6 and roast the laver for 5 minutes. Add Parmesan and basil to the quinoa risotto and sprinkle roasted laver on top.

● QUICHE WITH SPINACH, GREEN ASPARAGUS AND DULSE

Serves 4 / 2 hours

THE BASE
250 g spelt flour
½ tsp sea salt
125 g butter
1 egg
2 tbsp cold water

Put flour and salt in a large bowl. Rub the butter into the flour with your fingers until the mixture is like breadcrumbs. Mix in 1 egg and 2 tablespoons of cold water to give you a smooth dough. Knead it well and leave in a cool place for one hour. Preheat the oven to 200°C/400°F/gas 6. Knead the dough again and roll it to fit a 26-cm pie tin.

Chill for 30 minutes, covered with cling film. Cut a large piece of baking parchment and use to line the chilled pastry case, then tip in baking beans with more against the sides, to support the pastry wall when baking. Bake on a baking sheet for 15-20 minutes until the sides are crisp and set. Remove from the oven and carefully lift paper and beans out. Return pastry to oven and cook for another 5 minutes or until the base and sides are golden and crisp.

THE FILLING
1 tbsp olive oil
1 onion, finely chopped
500 g cleaned green asparagus cut into bites
150 g spinach, coarsely chopped
15 g dulse
3 eggs
250 ml milk
50 g Parmesan, freshly grated
50 g mild Edam cheese, freshly grated
Freshly grated nutmeg
Salt and pepper
1 pie dish with a loose base, 20 cm in diameter

Fry the onion and asparagus in the oil for 3 minutes, add spinach and dulse. Whisk 3 eggs with the cheese and the milk. Season to taste with salt, pepper and a pinch of grated nutmeg. Divide the fried vegetables evenly over the pastry and pour over the egg mixture. Lower the heat to 180°C/350°F/gas 4 and continue cooking for a further 25-30 minutes, or until the mixture is set.

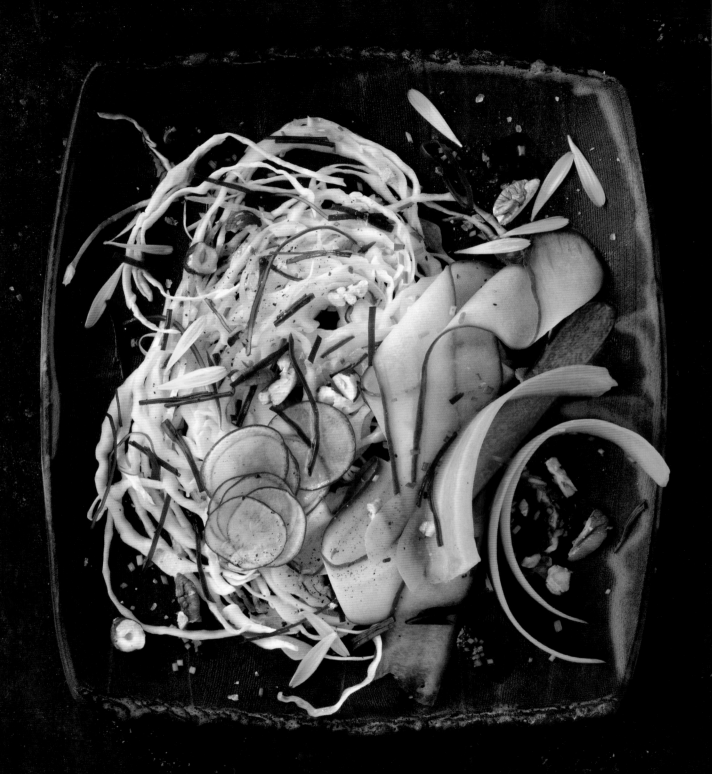

● RAW VEGETABLE SALAD

Serves 4 / 2 hours

MARINADE
20 g oarweed
2 tsp honey
1 tsp soy sauce
1 tbsp olive oil
1 garlic clove, chopped
2 tsp lime juice

DRESSING
1 tbsp sesame seed oil
2 tsp orange and pistachio spice (see recipe page 55)
2 tsp white rice vinegar
10 g fresh coriander
½ tsp salt

1 carrot, peeled and thinly sliced
15 small radishes, thinly sliced
150 g cabbage, thinly sliced
100 g cucumber, thinly sliced
25 g pecan nuts
25 g hazelnuts

TOPPING
A few marigold petals

Leave the oarweed to soak in water for one hour. Drain and cut into thin strips. Mix honey, soy sauce, olive oil, garlic and lime juice to a marinade. Leave the prepared oarweed to infuse in the marinade for a further one hour. Mix the dressing. Mix with the vegetables and nuts, adding the dressing and oarweed. Decorate with marigold petals.

● LAVER FALAFEL

Serves 4 / 1 hour (without soaking)

400 g dried chickpeas
30 g dried laver
½ bunch parsley, chopped
1 tsp harissa
½ tsp dried oregano
½ tsp ground cumin
1 tbsp sesame seeds
1 garlic clove, finely chopped
1 tbsp olive oil

Soak the chickpeas in cold water overnight. Boil the laver in water for 20 minutes. Place drained chickpeas, harissa, oregano, cumin, laver, parsley, sesame seeds and garlic in a food processor. Blend to a smooth paste. Scrape out the chickpea paste and shape it into 12 buns with dry hands. Pour a tablespoon of olive oil into the frying pan, add the chickpea buns, press them down a little with a fork and fry them until golden with a crisp crust on both sides.

YOGHURT DRESSING
200 g yoghurt
4 stalks fresh mint, chopped
1 garlic clove, chopped
Juice of 1 lime
1 tsp seaweed dukkah (see recipe page 55)

Mix yoghurt, chopped mint, garlic, lime juice and seaweed dukkah. Serve the falafel with yoghurt dressing. Tastes delicious with a tomato salad.

OYSTERS WITH DULSE

Serves 4 / 15 minutes

---

8 oysters
1-2 tbsp lime juice
4 tsp dulse flakes

Hold the oysters in a towel and open the shells with
an oyster knife or a small knife. Dress the oyster with
lime juice and sprinkle dulse flakes on top.

Eat the oysters the day you buy them, and serve them
on a bed of crushed ice.

●● ASPARAGUS RISOTTO WITH TOMATOES

Serves 4 / 1 hour

4 tbsp olive oil
60 g butter
1 onion, chopped
1 stalk celery, finely chopped
3 garlic cloves, finely chopped
350 g risotto rice
200 ml white wine
1 litre vegetable stock (see recipe page 81)
2 pieces oarweed
Salt
80 g gorgonzola
500 g green asparagus, peeled and cut into bites
  (break off the woody end)
400 g cherry tomatoes
1 tsp orange and pistachio spice (see recipe page 55)
1 tsp seabelt flakes
Fresh cress

Heat 2 tablespoons of olive oil and 30 g butter, add onion, celery and half of the garlic. Fry it while stirring for approx. 5 minutes without it colouring. Add the rice and continue to stir for a further one minute until the rice is shiny and translucent. Pour in the white wine and 100 ml of the vegetable stock and continue to stir. Add the oarweed.
Continue to add stock until the rice is tender, but with a slightly hard centre. Add a good pinch of salt. Add the asparagus for the last 5 minutes. Remove the saucepan from the heat, add 30 g butter and gorgonzola. Leave the dish to rest for 5 minutes.

Fry tomatoes and the rest of the garlic in 2 tablespoons of olive oil for 5 minutes. Season the risotto to taste with orange and pistachio spice and seabelt flakes. Remove the oarweed. Serve the dish decorated with fresh cress.

●● BRANDADE WITH DRIED COD AND SEAWEED
Serves 4 / 2 hours

300 g dried cod
150 g potatoes, peeled and cut into chunks
2 garlic cloves
100 ml milk
100 ml cream
50 ml olive oil
Pinch of grated nutmeg

HALF-DRIED TOMATOES
500 g cherry tomatoes
3 tbsp olive oil
1 tsp dried thyme
Seaweed salt
Seabelt flakes
7 g laver flakes

Soak the dried cod in cold water for at least 24-36 hours. Change the water 5-8 times. For the half-dried tomatoes: Mix tomatoes, oil, thyme, seaweed salt and seabelt flakes. Place everything in an ovenproof dish and leave to dry overnight in the oven at its lowest setting. Pour the milk and the cream into a saucepan with the garlic. Cut the pre-soaked cod into 5 cm pieces and mix the fish and potatoes with the cream mixture. Leave the fish to cook over low heat for approx. 30 minutes until the fish and the potatoes are tender and the fish cooked through. Remove the saucepan from the heat and leave it all to cool. Pour the liquid off the fish and the potatoes and keep for later. Blend fish, potatoes, olive oil, nutmeg and half of the liquid in a food processor.

Add more liquid to taste, if necessary. Serve the brandade on toasted sourdough bread, or other good bread, with half-dried tomatoes, seaweed salt and a sprinkle of laver.

●● CRAB AND LIME SALAD

Serves 4 / 35 minutes

20 g winged kelp, soaked in water for 10 minutes
4 tbsp olive oil
2 limes (organic, grated zest of 1 lime and
    the juice of both limes)
1 tsp mustard
1 tsp honey
1 tsp seaweed dukkah (see recipe page 55)
Pepper
200 g mixed green salad (beetroot leaves, mizuna,
    rocket, baby spinach)
300 g crab meat

Boil the winged kelp in water for 10 minutes. Rinse in
cold water and cut into thin strips. Shake together a
dressing of oil, lime zest, lime juice, mustard, honey,
seaweed dukkah and pepper in a glass jar with a
close-fitting lid. Mix a third of the dressing and the
winged kelp and leave to infuse for 1 hour. Mix a
third of the dressing with the crab meat. Arrange the
salad in bowls and place the marinated winged kelp
and crab meat on top.
Drizzle the rest of the dressing over the salad.

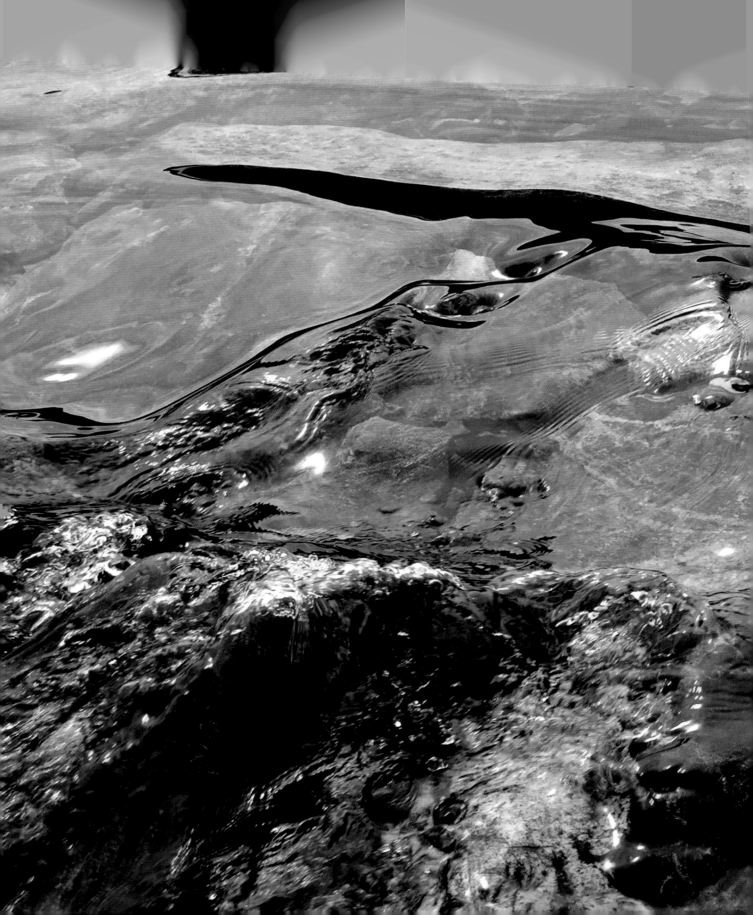

● PIZZA FRUTTI DI MARE
Serves 4 / 1 hour and 30 minutes

DOUGH
400 g spelt flour
100 g semolina
3 g flakes of laver or nori
1 tbsp olive oil
1 tsp salt
20 g fresh yeast
300 ml warm water

Mix the yeast in the warm water. Mix flour, semolina, nori flakes (or laver), olive oil and salt in a large bowl. Work in all the liquid with the dry ingredients. Knead the dough thoroughly until soft, even and elastic. Leave in a warm place for 20 minutes. Preheat the oven to 240° C/475°F/gas 9.

TOMATO SAUCE
2 tomatoes
1 garlic clove
1 tsp chipotle Tabasco
1 tbsp tomato purée
2 tbsp olive oil
2 tsp mild paprika
Salt and pepper

Coarsely blend all the ingredients in a food processor. Set the sauce aside.

TOPPING
250 g fish fillet, cut into slices
150 g mussels, cleaned
800 g crayfish, cleaned
7 g laver
350 g mozzarella, in slices
200 g green olives, in rings
70 g pea sprouts

Roll out the dough into a 26-cm circle and put on an oiled baking sheet or pizza stone, spread a little tomato sauce over the base and place crayfish, fish, mussels and laver on top. Cook the pizza until golden for approx. 8 minutes. Arrange the mozzarella and the olives on the pizza and cook for a further 2 minutes until the cheese has melted. Sprinkle pea sprouts over the pizza and serve immediately.

CALZONE WITH DULSE

1 hour and 30 minutes

DOUGH
1 tsp dried yeast
300 ml lukewarm water
1 tsp sugar
1 tsp salt
450 g spelt flour
2 tbsp olive oil

FILLING
2 tomatoes, sliced,
200 g mozzarella, sliced
30 g spinach, chopped
20 g dulse
2 spring onions, cut into rings
1 egg, whisked

Mix the yeast into a little lukewarm water in a large bowl. Leave for 5 minutes. Add sugar, salt, and half the flour. Mix everything at a gentle and low speed with an electric hand mixer to a smooth paste. Gradually stir in the rest of the flour and the olive oil until you have a soft dough.
Place the dough in a well greased bowl, turn the dough and grease it on the other side too. Cover the dough and leave it to rise in a warm place for one hour or until it has almost doubled in size. Preheat the oven to 190°C/375°F/gas 5. Knead the dough thoroughly and divide it into 4 pieces. Roll each piece to a thin, round base, approx. 15 cm diameter.

Cover half of each piece of dough with tomatoes, cheese, spinach, dulse and spring onions. Fold the dough over the filling and seal the calzone by pressing the edges down with a fork. Brush the calzones with whisked egg and place them on a lightly greased baking sheet. Put the calzones in the oven and cook until golden for 25 minutes.

● SLOW-COOKED COD PARCELS IN WINGED KELP

Serves 4 / 1 hour

15 g winged kelp
3 tbsp olive oil
½ small red onion, coarsely chopped
100 g red pepper, cut into cubes
1 garlic clove, crushed
2 g saffron
1 tbsp mild, smoked paprika
700 g cod fillet
Seaweed salt with dulse and pepper
10 g pistachio nuts, toasted
3 tomatoes, sliced
Sprouts

Place the winged kelp to soak in water for at least
1 hour. Preheat the oven to 150°C/300°F/gas 2. Blend
2 tbsp olive oil, red onion, red pepper, garlic, saffron
and smoked paprika to a smooth paste in a food
processor. Set aside. Divide the fish into 4 portions,
season with sea salt and pepper, rub each fillet with
the spice paste, sprinkle pistachio nuts over and roll
each one in separate leaves of winged kelp.
Set aside. Place the sliced tomatoes in an oven dish
and arrange the fish parcels on top. Add the rest of the
olive oil, seaweed salt with dulse and pepper. Cook
the fish parcels in the oven for 30 to 40 minutes. Serve
the cod with or without the winged kelp. Sprinkle a
few sprouts over the top before serving.

● BLACK RICE SALAD
Serves 4 / 1 hour and 30 minutes

---

100 g black or wild rice
500 ml vegetable stock (see recipe page 81)
Juice and zest of 1 lemon
4 g fresh ginger, grated
2 tbsp honey
1 Indian Long Pepper, crushed
1 tbsp sea salt
4 tbsp rice vinegar
6 tbsp tamari sauce
2 tbsp sesame seed oil
2 tbsp olive oil
200 g almond and sesame tofu (or any other sort),
   cut into cubes
2 g oarweed
50 g baby spinach leaves
1 shallot, chopped
40 g seaweed dukkah (see recipe page 55)
¼ handful coriander, chopped
1 spring onion, finely chopped
Pecan nuts

Cook the rice with the stock for approx. 35 minutes over low and gentle heat. For the dressing: Mix lemon zest, lemon juice, ginger, honey, long pepper, sea salt, rice vinegar and tamari in a blender. Add sesame seed oil and 1 tablespoon olive oil a little at a time.

Preheat the oven to 200°C/400°F/gas 6. Fry the tofu in a frying pan with 1 tablespoon oil. Place the oarweed to soak in cold water for approx. 5 minutes. Pour off the water and roast the oarweed in the oven for 5 minutes before crushing it coarsely. Mix rice, spinach, shallot, pecan nuts, seaweed dukkah, coriander, spring onions and dressing. Sprinkle seaweed and tofu over the salad just before serving.

●● CASHEW BALLS WITH GRAPES

Serves 6-8 / 1 hour

400 g cashew nuts
4 tbsp psyllium husks
150 ml water
2 tbsp lemon juice
½ tsp salt
5 g white sesame seeds
5 g black sesame seeds
1 g dulse flakes
1 g dulse, chopped
1 g seabelt flakes
1 g nori flakes

TOPPING
500 g black or red grapes

Soak the cashew nuts in water for approx. 2 hours.
Mix the psyllium husks and 150 ml water in a bowl to
a paste. Pour off the water from the nuts. Blend
cashew nuts, psyllium paste, lemon juice and salt to a
soft dough in a food processor. Leave the dough to
rest for 10 minutes. Mix the rest of the ingredients
(apart from the grapes) in a bowl. Form small balls
from the dough and roll them in the seaweed
mixture. Serve the balls with grapes on the side.

●●● CEVICHE WITH MANGO AND TOMATO

Serves 4 / 35 minutes

2 mangoes, peeled and coarsely chopped
90 g red cherry tomatoes, cut in half
90 g yellow cherry tomatoes, cut in half
2 small green tomatoes, cut into wedges
1 avocado, peeled and coarsely chopped
1 red onion, cut into rings
75 g sugar snaps
1 stalk celery, cut on the slant
200 g cod, cut into large chunks

DRESSING
1 tbsp lemon juice
1 tbsp lime juice
1 tbsp avocado oil
1 tsp chopped ginger
1 tsp chopped garlic
1 tsp jalapeño chilli sauce
1 tsp chopped coriander
1 tsp seabelt flakes
½ tsp sea salt

TOPPING
4 g laver flakes
Lime zest in strips (only the green bits)
Pea shoots
Crushed pepper

Mix all the ingredients carefully in a large bowl and
arrange in 4 soup bowls. Make the dressing, pour it
over the ceviche and take care that everything is
covered by the dressing. Garnish the ceviche and
serve immediately.

TAGLIATELLE WITH SEA LETTUCE PESTO AND BLUEBERRIES

Serves 4 / 1 hour

PESTO
150 ml olive oil
1 garlic clove, coarsely chopped
3 tbsp sea lettuce flakes
150 g pistachio nuts (or other nuts)
2 handfuls of coriander
1 tbsp lemon juice
1 tsp salt

BALSAMIC BLUEBERRIES
50 ml balsamic vinegar
50 ml water
1 tbsp brown sugar
150 g blueberries
Crushed black pepper
500 g tagliatelle

TOPPING
2 g roasted thongweed, coarsely chopped
A few coriander leaves

Place all the ingredients for the pesto in a blender.
Boil the balsamic vinegar, water and sugar in a small
saucepan until a quarter of the original quantity
remains, then add blueberries and crushed pepper.
Boil the tagliatelle to al dente in 1.5 litres boiling
water. Top the pasta with the pesto and blueberries
and serve immediately.

● FISH'N'CHIPS

Serves 4 / 1 hour

500 g large potatoes
3 tbsp olive oil
1 pinch of seaweed salt
2 tsp dried thyme
150 g rice flour, plus extra for dusting
150 ml water
1 tsp lemon juice
½ tsp baking powder
1 egg
400 g fish fillet (cod or pollock)
10 g seabelt flakes
200 ml cooking oil for deep frying

Wash the potatoes thoroughly and cut them into wedges. Place them in a roasting tin and pour over 3 tbsp oil. Mix well. Sprinkle with a little seaweed salt and thyme. Cook the potatoes at 220°C/425°F/gas 7 for 20 minutes until the potatoes are crisp and with a golden crust. Use a sharp knife to test whether the potatoes are cooked. Whisk together a batter of rice flour, 150 ml water, salt, lemon juice, baking powder and egg. Cut the fish fillets into 2 cm pieces. Coat the fish pieces in a little rice flour, dip them in the batter and finally turn them in seabelt flakes. Heat the oil in a saucepan. Fry the fish and serve it with the oven-baked potato wedges, aioli (see recipe page 101) and a little lemon juice squeezed over.

● CARROT AND GINGER SOUP
Serves 4 / 1 hour

PARSLEY OIL
1 bunch parsley
150 ml olive oil
1 stalk tarragon, chopped

Blanch the parsley in boiling water for 3 minutes. Cool in ice-cold water. Pat it dry with kitchen towel. Coarsely chop the parsley and mix it with tarragon and olive oil. Set the parsley oil aside.

SOUP
2 tbsp olive oil
1 leek, cut into chunks
250 g carrots, cut into chunks
50 g red lentils
350 ml vegetable stock (see recipe page 81)
150 ml orange juice
Pinch grated nutmeg
1 tsp cumin
1 tbsp fresh ginger, grated
½ tsp mustard seed
1 tbsp turmeric
Seaweed salt
250 ml coconut milk

Heat 2 tbsp olive oil in a frying pan and fry the leek until golden. Add carrots, red lentils, vegetable stock, orange juice and spices. Leave to simmer for approx. 30 minutes.
Mix in a blender to a smooth paste. Add the coconut milk and leave the soup to simmer at low heat for a further 5 minutes.

TOPPING
2 garlic cloves, cut into strips
2 tbsp olive oil
1 tbsp seabelt flakes

Heat 1 tbsp olive oil in a frying pan and fry the garlic. Serve the soup with parsley oil, fried garlic and seabelt flakes.

POTATO AND CELERIAC MASH WITH DULSE, SPINACH AND FRIED SWEET POTATO STRIPS

Serves 4 / 1hour

500 g potatoes, peeled and cut into large chunks
300 g celeriac, peeled and cut into large chunks
3 tbsp olive oil
2 tbsp lemon juice
Salt
1 pinch freshly ground nutmeg
20 g butter
Zest of 1 lemon (organic)
2 garlic cloves, chopped
1 onion, finely chopped
1 red chilli, finely chopped
500 g spinach
20 g dulse
Pepper
1 tsp orange and pistachio spice
    (see recipe page 55)
150 ml vegetable oil
200 g sweet potatoes, peeled and thinly sliced
    into strips
1 tbsp ground pistachio nuts
Sprinkle of dulse

Place potatoes and celeriac in a medium saucepan. Add cold water until it covers the potatoes and the celeriac by approx. 3 cm. Turn up the heat and bring to the boil. Then turn down and simmer the potatoes and celeriac until tender over low heat. Pour off the water and mash the potato and celeriac mixture with a fork. Add olive oil, lemon juice, salt and nutmeg.

Melt the butter in a large frying pan and add lemon zest, garlic, onion and chilli. Add spinach and dulse and mix until the spinach has wilted. Season to taste with salt, pepper and orange and pistachio spice. Heat the vegetable oil in a small saucepan. Fry the sweet potato strips without stirring for 2-3 minutes until they are golden. Remove from the oil with a perforated skimmer and leave to dry on a chopping board lined with kitchen towel. Serve everything together and sprinkle a few dulse flakes and ground pistachio nuts on top.

●● REDFISH WRAPPED IN WINGED KELP

Serves 4 / 1hour

HUMMUS
250 g chickpeas, cooked
10 g fresh ginger, grated
2 garlic cloves, finely chopped
4 tbsp lemon juice
2 g seabelt flakes
1 tbsp turmeric
1 tbsp agave syrup

FISH
11 g winged kelp
750 g redfish fillet
1 garlic clove, chopped
Zest of 1 lemon (organic)
1 tsp chilli paste
Salt and pepper
30 g butter

TOPPING
1 lime, thinly sliced
1 small chilli, thinly sliced
Fresh sprouts

Place the winged kelp in water to soak for at least 1 hour and remove the stalk in the middle. Set the kelp aside. Blend all the ingredients for the hummus in a food processor to a smooth paste. Set aside. Cut the redfish fillets into 4 portions and rub each fillet with lemon zest, garlic, chilli paste, salt and pepper. Wrap each fish fillet in a winged kelp leaf. Set the fish parcels aside. Melt the butter in a hot frying pan and add the fish parcels. Fry for approx. 6 minutes on each side. Remove the fish parcels from the pan and set aside.

Place lime slices and chopped chilli in the glaze of juices in the frying pan for approx. 30 seconds. Arrange the lime slices on a serving dish and place the fish parcels on top. Pour over a little of the spicy glaze from the pan. Serve the hummus in individual dishes. Top with sprouts and chilli.

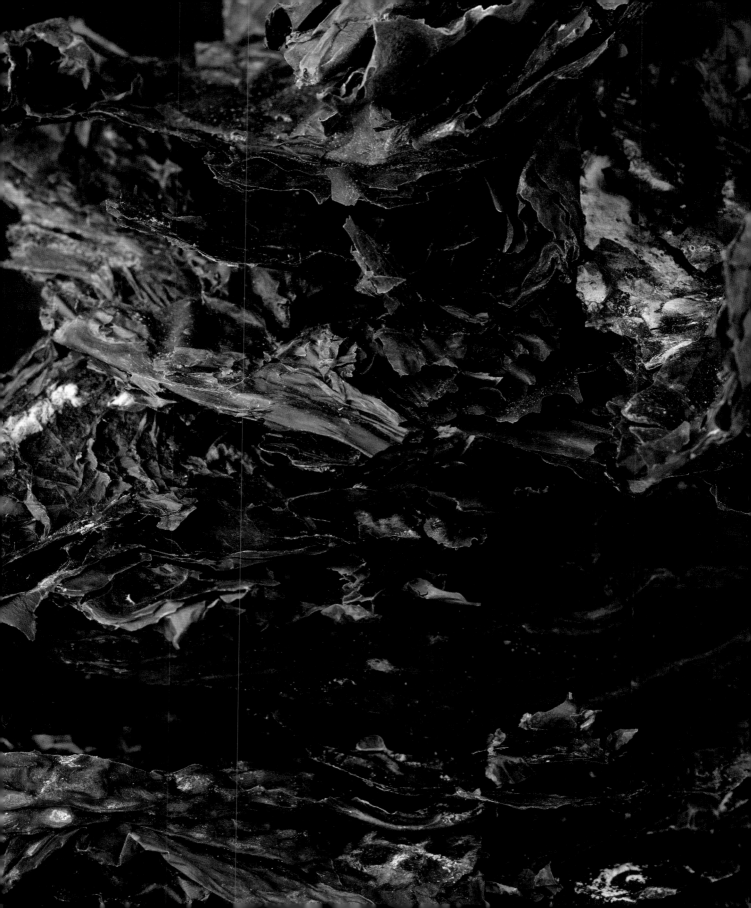

●● CREAMY SOUP WITH BOLETUS MUSHROOMS

Serves 4 / 35 minutes

400 g boletus mushrooms or other mushrooms
    (for example Sweet Tooth or Chanterelle), cleaned
    and cut into cubes
2 tbsp olive oil or 30 g butter
1 leek, chopped
2 garlic cloves, chopped
200 g potatoes, peeled and cut into cubes
1 litre mushroom stock (see recipe on page 81)
2 pieces oarweed
100 ml cream
Fresh or dried thyme, chopped
1 tsp seaweed salt with dulse
Pepper
1 tsp dulse flakes
A few dulse leaves

TOPPING
A few marigold petals

Cook the mushroom cubes in a dry frying pan and let
them release their juices. Set aside. Heat the oil in a
saucepan and fry leek, garlic and potatoes. Add stock
and oarweed and bring to the boil. Turn down the
heat and leave to simmer for approx. 20 minutes over
low heat. Remove the oarweed. Add mushroom cubes
and juices, cream and thyme and blend in a blender.
Reheat the soup. Season to taste with seaweed salt,
pepper and dulse flakes. Garnish the soup with petals
of marigold flowers.

●● CHOCOLATE BALLS

Serves 4 / 40 minutes

---

25 g coconut sugar (or brown sugar)
75 ml coconut milk
75 g mixed nuts
1 g seabelt flakes
75 g chocolate
1 g dulse flakes

Cook coconut sugar and coconut milk to a soft
toffee. Add the nuts and seabelt and mix in. Shape
the paste into 15 balls. Melt the chocolate and cover
the balls with chocolate. Sprinkle a little seabelt and
dulse on top.

● CRUMBLE PIE WITH BERRIES, DULSE AND BALSAMIC VINEGAR

Serves 4 / 1 hour and 20 minutes

---

420 g blueberries (or other berries)

MARINADE
4 tbsp balsamic vinegar
6 tbsp water
4 tbsp agave syrup
5 g dulse
10 g sugar

DOUGH
50 g ground almonds
60 g spelt flour
45 g brown sugar
½ tsp ground ginger
1 pinch of salt
60 g cold butter

Preheat the oven to 200°C/400°F/gas 6. Mix all the
ingredients for the marinade with blueberries and
leave to infuse for approx. 20 minutes. Mix ground
almonds, spelt flour, brown sugar, ginger and salt for
the crumble in a bowl. Cut the cold butter into small
pieces and rub it into the dry mixture with your
fingertips until you have a mixture a little like
breadcrumbs. Set aside. Arrange the berries in an
ovenproof dish, pour over the marinade and cover
with the crumble. Cook the pie for 20-25 minutes
until golden. Sprinkle with sugar before serving.

SWEET CHOCOLATE AND BEETROOT CAKE WITH VANILLA ICE CREAM WRAPPED IN DULSE

Serves 4 / 1 hour and 20 minutes

150 g dark chocolate
120 g butter
80 g flour
100 g ground almonds
1 tsp baking powder
20 g dulse
¼ tsp ground cinnamon
1 scant tsp ground cardamom
5 free-range eggs
50 g honey
250 g beetroot, peeled and grated
200 ml vanilla ice cream

Preheat the oven to 180° C/350°F/gas 4. Melt the chocolate and butter in a saucepan over low heat. Whisk flour, ground almond, baking powder, 10 g dulse, cinnamon and cardamom in a large bowl. Set aside. In another bowl whisk eggs and honey with an electric hand mixer until light and airy. With the mixer at low speed add the flour mixture, grated beetroot and melted chocolate very gradually. Whisk until it is thoroughly mixed. Grease 4 12-cm cake tins with oil and pour the batter into the tins. Bake the cakes for 25-30 minutes. (Insert a wooden skewer into the middle of the cake. It must come out clean, but a little damp, when you take it out.) Wrap the ice cream in dulse (10 g) and serve the ice cream with the cakes.

TOFFEE AND DULSE ICE CREAM WITH PISTACHIO AND DULSE CHOCOLATE

Serves 4 / 1 hour and 20 minutes

150 g sugar
250 g milk
250 g cream
¼ tsp sea salt
10 g dulse
1 vanilla pod, cut lengthwise
4 free-range eggs
100 g ground pistachio nuts
100 g dark chocolate
2 tsp dulse flakes

TOPPING
A few petals from marigold flowers

Scrape the seeds from the vanilla pod and set aside. Heat the sugar in a dry, thick-based saucepan over medium-hot heat until the sugar starts to melt. Turn the saucepan now and then to ensure that the sugar melts evenly. Continue until the sugar has turned dark golden. Add the milk and cream (this will splutter in the pan), and cook the mixture while constantly stirring until all the sugar is dissolved. Pour the mixture into a bowl and mix in sea salt and 10 g dulse and the vanilla seeds. Cool at room temperature. Whisk the eggs in a medium-sized bowl. Add the warm milk mixture in a thin drizzle while constantly whisking. Pour the mixture back into the saucepan and heat it over medium heat while constantly stirring with a wooden spoon until the mixture sticks to the back of the spoon (it should not boil). Sieve the mixture into a large bowl through a fine mesh sieve. Place the bowl with the ice cream in the deep freezer for 4 hours. Stir the mixture every half hour, to prevent ice crystals forming in the ice cream. Melt the chocolate in a bain marie while constantly stirring. Pour the chocolate onto a baking tray covered with baking paper.

Sprinkle dulse flakes over. Let the chocolate set for several hours at room temperature until completely set. You can also set the baking tray in the fridge, to speed up the setting process. Serve the ice cream with chocolate and ground pistachio nuts and sprinkle dulse flakes and a few marigold petals on top.

●● GIN SEAWEED TONIC, SEABELT MARTINI

Serves 4 / 5 minutes

GIN SEAWEED TONIC
200 ml gin
600 ml tonic water
4 dulse leaves
Ice cubes

Place the ice cubes and dulse in 4 glasses. Add gin and tonic water and serve the drink immediately.

SEABELT MARTINI
120 ml dry vermouth
240 ml gin
4 pieces seabelt
Ice cubes

Chill the cocktail glasses. Fill a metal shaker with crushed ice. Pour in the dry vermouth, shake it lightly.
Add gin, shake vigorously for approx. 10 seconds, pour the drink into pre-chilled glasses and garnish with seabelt.

● POLENTA STICKS WITH PAPRIKA DIP AND ALMOND STICKS

Serves 4 / 1 hour

POLENTA STICKS

400 ml vegetable stock (see recipe page 81)
2 garlic cloves
5 g winged kelp, first soaked, then cut into
   smaller pieces
200 g instant polenta (coarse cornflour)
30 g grated Parmesan
3 g rosemary
2 tbsp olive oil
1 tbsp seaweed dukkah (see recipe page 55)

Bring stock, garlic and winged kelp to the boil in a saucepan, add the polenta and cook until it leaves the edge of the saucepan. Add Parmesan, rosemary and seaweed dukkah towards the end of the cooking time.

Spread the paste over a baking sheet lined with baking paper and leave to cool. Cut the polenta in suitable strips, sprinkle the oil over the mixture and bake in the oven for 15 minutes at 220°C/425°F/gas 7.

PEPPER DIP

½ red pepper, cut into small chunks
1 skinless tomato, seeds removed
1 tbsp agave syrup
1 tsp rice vinegar
½ garlic clove, chopped
2 tbsp olive oil
20 basil leaves
Salt and pepper
Dulse flakes

Roast the pepper chunks. Mix all the ingredients in a blender. Sprinkle a few dulse flakes on top before serving.

ALMOND STICKS

2 tbsp chia seeds
200 g ground almonds
2 tbsp seabelt flakes
1 tbsp olive oil
1 tsp orange and pistachio spice (see recipe page 55)

Mix the chia seeds with 8 tablespoons water and leave the seeds to infuse in the water for 1 hour. Then mix chia seeds, ground almonds, seabelt flakes and 1 teaspoon of the spice mix. Form the paste into sticks and bake in the oven for 10 minutes at 200°C/400°F/gas 6.

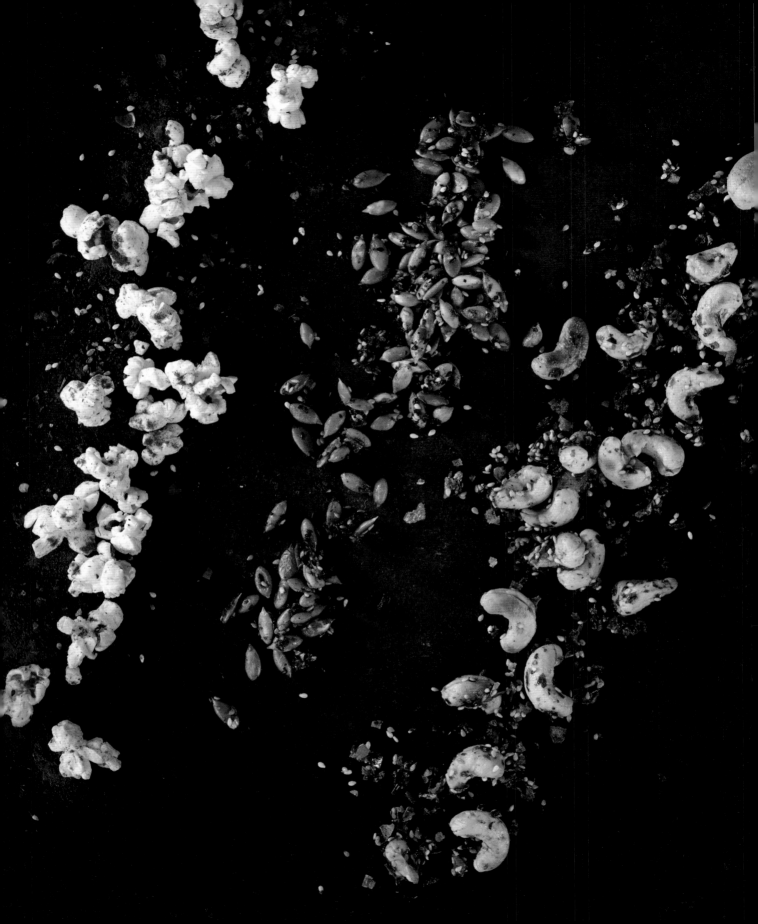

● CASHEW SNACKS, PUMPKIN SEEDS AND SEAWEED POPCORN

20 minutes

CASHEW SNACKS

100 g raw cashew nuts
½ tsp ground turmeric
1 tsp sesame seed oil
1 g seabelt flakes
1 tsp sesame seeds
Pinch of salt
1 Indian Long Pepper or 5 black peppercorns

Fry the cashew nuts and turmeric in sesame seed oil
in a frying pan and roast the seabelt flakes separately
in the oven. Fry the sesame seeds. Grind pepper,
sesame seeds, salt and seabelt in a mortar.
Mix the cashew nuts with the pepper mixture.

PUMPKIN SEEDS

150 g pumpkin seeds
1 tsp white sesame seeds
1 tsp black sesame seeds
1 tbsp agave syrup
2 tsp olive oil
Pinch of chilli
1 tbsp dulse flakes

Roast all the ingredients in a pan.

SEAWEED POPCORN

3 tbsp canola oil
100 g unpopped popcorn
30 g butter, melted
Pinch of seaweed salt
1 tsp smoked paprika
2 tbsp seabelt flakes

Heat the oil in a saucepan over medium heat. Add the
popcorn. It will soon begin to pop. When the popping
starts, shake the saucepan slightly by pulling it
backwards and forwards over the heat and cover with
a lid. Try to keep the lid a little loose to let the steam
escape. This will make the popcorn drier and crisper.
Pour the popcorn into a bowl. Add melted butter,
seaweed salt, paprika and seabelt flakes.

INDEX

DIRECTORY OF RESOURCES

The fantastic properties of seaweed as food and a sustainable raw ingredient is no longer a well kept secret. There are many people who are working with seaweed and kelp and who are making a fantastic effort to spread the knowledge.
On these pages is collected information about dealers and selected resources.
The following links include most of what you need to know about seaweed as a food and raw material resource.
We particularly recommend Ole G. Mouritsen's wonderful book *Seaweeds: Edible, Available & Sustainable* seaweedbook.net
The most complete, the biggest and oldest information page about seaweed and kelp: seaweed.ie

PRODUCERS FOR HUMAN CONSUMPTION

Seagreens®
1 The Warren
Handcross
West Sussex RH17 6DX
Great Britain

t. +44 1444 400403
info@seagreens.co.uk
www.seagreens.co.uk

Just Seaweed
18A Argyle Street
Rothesay
Isle of Bute
Western Isles PA20 0AU
Scotland
t. +44 1700 505823
justseaweed@gmail.com
www.justseaweed.com

Clearspring
19A Acton Park Estate
London W3 7QE
Great Britain
t. +44 20 8749 1781
info@clearspring.co.uk
www.clearspring.co.uk

Cornish Seaweed Company
Higher Argal Farm
Falmouth
Cornwall TR11 5PE
Great Britain
t. +44 1326 618469
info@cornishseaweed.co.uk
www.cornishseaweed.co.uk

Connemara Organic Seaweed
Unit 3, Rossaveal
County Galway H91X F2H
Ireland
t. +353 91 506848
noel@connemaraseaweedcompany.ie
www.connemaraseaweedcompany.ie

Lofoten Seaweed Company
Solhøgdveien 16
8382 Napp i Lofoten
Norway
t. +47 90 673522
angelita@lofotenseaweed.com
www.facebook.com/lofoten-seaweed-company-331647650562119

Acadian Seaplants
30 Brown Avenue
Dartmouth
Nova Scotia B38 1XB
Canada
t. +1 902 468 2840
info@acadian.ca
www.acadianseaplants.com

Maine Coast Sea Vegetables
430 Washington Junction Road
Hancock
Maine ME 04640, USA
t. +1 207 412 0094

info@seaveg.com
www.seaveg.com

NON PROFIT AND CHARITABLE

Seaweed Health Foundation
The Warren
Handcross
West Sussex RH17 6DX
Great Britain
t. +44 1444 400403
post@seaweedhealthfoundation.co.uk
www.seaweedhealthfoundation.org.uk

British Phycological Society
Natural History Museum
Cromwell Road
London SW7 5BD
Great Britain
t. +44 1947 605501
secretary@brphycsoc.org
www.brphycsoc.org

AlgaeBase
Ryan Institute
National University of Ireland
University Road
Galway
Ireland
www.algaebase.org

Marine Life Information Network
The Marine Biological
Association of the UK
Citadel Hill
Plymouth
Devon PL1 2PB
t. +44 1752 426543
marlin@mba.ac.uk
www.marlin.ac.uk

SEAWEED PRODUCT SPECIALIST
RETAILERS

Oceans of Goodness
4 Springfield Road
Southgate
Crawley
West Sussex RH11 8AD
Great Britain
t. +44 1293 520460
seaweed@oceansofgoodness.co.uk
www.oceansofgoodness.co.uk

Seaweed Heaven
4 Springfield Road
Crawley
West Sussex RH11 8AD
Great Britain
t. +44 1293 520460
www.seaweedheaven.co.uk

Seagreens USA
International Nutrition Suite T
11655 Crossroads Circle
Middle River
Maryland MD 211220
USA
ask@seagreensonline.com
www.seagreensonline.com

Gaps Nutrition
12A Whitehall Avenue
St James Park
Birkdale
Queensland QLD 4159
Australia
t. +61 40 909 9758
contact@gapsaustralia.com.au
www.gapsaustralia.com.au

THANK YOU

Anne Berit Tuft, Vidar Grimshei and all the others at Cappelen Damm who believed and took the chance on a very different book. Tina Holth for invaluable assistance, kindness and support. Knut Bry for having a love of nature in our elongated country and for allowing us to use the pictures in the book. Henrik Berg Slang for contributing with the words we did not have. Tom Bråten for being our technical spine and unwavering rock from the tentative beginning to the hectic end. Lars Petter Pettersen for fabulous dignified portrait photos of the writers. Tone Dahl for invaluable quality assurance of content.
Sarah Willoch for having steely control of grid and paragraph related challenges. Kate Hagen and Lis Madeleine Lonning for having held our hands during the design project. Emma Olsen, Anne Gro Carlsson, Charlotte Kristoffersen, Halvor Bodin, Claudia Sandor, Baptiste Ringot, Thomas Sandsør, John Rørdam and Kent André Nøkleby for lending eyes, invaluable input, visual solutions and general inspiration.

Pedro Torres for feedback on the recipes and help for improvements. Simon Sturluson for taking us on seaweed harvesting in Iceland and for all the fresh raw materials. Grettir Hreinsson for the lovely seaweed products. Caxtalot for Swedish seaweed. The Northern Company for Norwegian seaweed. Siri Mathisen from Lindesnes fyr. Dronebrygg for dulse beer. Sandra Schollmeyer and Serax for help and loan of accessories/props. Beate Gauder, Marte Aubert and Lina Solberg for good relationships. Alex Asensi for photographs from Iceland and Træna.

An extra thank you to our friends and families for generally believing in us and for their patience through everything it takes to make a cookbook.

Claudia, Zoe, Lisa & Hanne

Grub Street wish to thank Simon Ranger of The Seaweed Health Foundation for his invaluable help in supplying the contacts in the Directory of Resources.